# ULTRA-PSYCHONICS:

## How to Work Miracles
## with the Limitless Power
## of Psycho-Atomic Energy

# ULTRA-PSYCHONICS:

## How to Work Miracles with the Limitless Power of Psycho-Atomic Energy

*by Walter Delaney*

PARKER PUBLISHING COMPANY, INC.

West Nyack, New York

**Library of Congress Cataloging in Publication Data**

Delaney, Walter
    Ultra-psychonics: how to work miracles with the
limitless power of psycho-atomic energy.

    1. Occult sciences. 2. Success. I. Title.
[DNLM: 1. Parapsychology--Popular works.  BF1031 D337u]
BF1999.D347      133          74-16232
ISBN 0-13-935635-5

Printed in the United States of America

*To Dorothy, Pinkie
and Cleo whose
encouragement and
help made this book
possible.*

# *What This Book Will Do for You*

How many times 'have you wished that your life could be better? How often have you wished there was a way you could get more of the good things of life—the fat bank accounts, the passionate love, the high honors, the deep admiration and respect that others seem to win almost without trying?

If you're tired of scrimping and saving for things you never seem able to afford, of working long hours for low wages, of begging and pleading to get things that should be rightfully yours, of always having to settle for "second best"—then this book is for you!

For in it, you will discover a whole new world—a world where miracles take place at your command—a world in which you are king and everyone else must bow to your wishes—a world, in short, where your most-cherished, most deeply-desired dreams are about to come true.

This is the world of Ultra-Psychonics—the amazing new way to use the limitless power of "psycho-atomic energy" to bring you the things you want.

## Surging Power Is at Your Command

In the first part of this unusual book, you're going to see how to release this mighty power. Step-by-step, in crystal-clear detail, you'll discover what "psycho-atomic energy" really is, how you can control it and how you can use it in scores of different ways for such things as materializing riches, finding lost relatives, invoking the secret forces of nature, improving your health, reading the minds of others, seeing into the future and much, much more.

Then, each branch of Ultra-Psychonics is mapped out for you,

7

and its secrets revealed in full. Nothing is held back, nothing is concealed—it's all placed right in your hands, ready to be used!

Quickly, easily, automatically . . . like rain falling on a parched desert . . . Ultra-Psychonic power will start to flow into you, transforming you into a dynamic, potent individual with abilities that stagger the imagination.

Here are just a few of the things you're about to discover:

- How to generate and release powerful streams of mental energy . . . Psychonic and Ultronic Laser Beams that can work wonders!

- How to use ultronically "loaded" words that make others obey you as if they were thought-controlled robots!

- How to seize control of people with just one flashing glance!

- How to create things out of thin air with "Ultra-Glyphics"!

- How "reverse money flow" can bring in cash faster than you can spend it!

- How to develop a mirror-perfect memory in just a few days!

- How to recall people, places and events from previous lives!

- How to use the amazing secret of "interstitial time" to s-t-r-e-t-c-h out your hours of pleasure, shorten your hours of work!

- How to multiply your brainpower 1,000 times practically overnight!

- How to improve your health with ultra-mitogenic rays!

- How to lengthen your lifespan with unusual vitamins and herbs!

- How to discover your sign in the new Psychonic Zodiac and read the invisible messages in the sky that can help you!

- How to set up an "astronic chart" that tells you amazing things about the people you know!

- How to build a new kind of dowsing rod that can turn up lost or buried treasure thousands of miles away!

- How to use a special "recovery chant" that summons back lost or stolen objects!
- How to defend yourself against your secret enemies with special spells, amulets and talismans!
- How to put together a remarkable "time machine" that brings you back information about the future!
- How to discover the master numbers that rule your life, and put them to work for you to make you a winner in whatever you try!
- How to use the startling secret of the "Power Primes" to find and captivate the people who can help you most!
- How to set up an Ultra-Telepathic Power Globe that lets you read the minds of others as if you were reading an open book!
- How to defend yourself against psychic attack!
- How to move objects with the force of your mind alone!
- How to become "invisible" and able to pass through solid walls!
- How to take possession of other people's bodies!
- How to achieve Cosmic Illumination and find true happiness and peace of mind!
- How to use a new, stronger kind of prayer that is extraordinarily effective!
- How to discover your true purpose in life and use it to create a wonderful new future for yourself!

. . . and that's only the beginning.

### The Lifetime Plan for Developing Your Ultra-Psychonic Power

Here, in effect, is a Lifetime Plan for you to discover, train, control and use your sleeping mental powers. It is a way for you to get the fundamental Laws of the Universe working for you, instead of against you. And it is yours for the asking.

"What *is* Ultra-Psychonics?" you ask.

It is a force beside which the mightiest bolt of lightning, the most enormous fire, the highest waterfall are like toys. It is a power that nothing can withstand—that sweeps everything before it as a hurricane blows dried leaves. And it is yours for the asking.

"Is it hard to learn?" you ask.

Not at all. It is as simple, easy and natural as breathing. It can be used by the young, the old, the rich and the poor alike. It works as well for women as it does for men, and it works for all races, religions and creeds. Sick or well, tall or short, fat or thin—Ultra-Psychonics will work for *you!* And it is yours for the asking.

"All right, I'm asking," you say. "How do I get started?"

Turn to Chapter 1 and start reading. That's all it takes. You don't have to read the whole book at once. Read a chapter a night—or even just a page—and see for yourself the wonders that Ultra-Psychonics can perform.

There's never been anything like it—and there may never be again. It's the dream of the ages, come at last. It is the climax of my life's work—my gift to mankind.

And it is yours for the asking.

*—Walter Delaney*

# Table of Contents

Chart - How to Get a Reading When You Have Only Partial Data -
How to Get a Quick On-the-Spot Reading in Less than Five
Minutes - What Ultra-Astronics Can Do for You

How Ultra-Divination Works - The Amazing Anti-Particles from
the Hidden Universe - How to Generate the Anti-Laser Beams - The
Secret of Anti-Egonic Flow - How to Charge Yourself with Ultra-
Divination Power - How Ward M. Found a Lost Will - Building a
Psychonic Radar Locator for Less than $1.00 - How Evelyn P.
Found 12 Oil Wells - Finding Things Underwater Using "Map .
Dowsing" - How Malcolm C. Located a Fortune in Pirate Gold
- How to Bring Back True Love - How Dinah B. Brought Back
Her Runaway Husband and Made Him Be True - The Astounding
"Miracle Map" That Finds Lost Relatives - How Ethel D. Found
Her Long-Lost Son and Brought Him Home - An Unusual Ultra-
Divination Technique for Finding Lost Pets - How Sam and
Irma Found Their Missing Cat - The Anti-Psychonic "Recovery
Chant" That Summons Back Lost or Stolen Objects - How
Marion T. Got Back Her Missing Jewelry - How to Make Money
Finding Things for Others-What Ultra-Divination Can Do for You.

The Astonishing Power of Ultra-Magic - The Mighty Power Behind
Ultra-Magic - Ultra-Magic Spells That Can Help You - The Magne-
tic Spell That Brings Friendship - The Magnetic Spell that Attracts
Good Luck - The Magnetic Love Spell That Never Fails - Spell
Brings Man to Her from 200 Miles Away - How to Defend Your-
self Against Black Magic and Witchcraft - Counter-Attacking a
Known Enemy - How Rudy Cured His Stomach Pains - Protecting
Yourself with Ultra-Magic Amulets - The Ultra-Magic Coin Amulet:
Ultimate Protection Against Evil - The Ultra-Magic Quick Amulet:
Fast Protection on Short Notice - The Ultra-Magic Home Amulet:
How to Protect Your Worldly Goods - Reading Signs and Omens
with Ultra-Magic - The Secret of the Cave - How to Recognize
Good and Bad Omens - Ultra-Demonology: Protection Against the
Forces of Evil - The Ceremony That Invokes Your Psychic Guar-
dian - What Ultra-Magic Can Do for You - Warning

Does the Future Already Exist? - Can the Future Be Changed? - How
Anti-Ultrons Flow Through Time - Building an Ultronic Time-
Machine - The Secret of Using Your Ultronic Time-Machine to

# ULTRA-PSYCHONICS:

## How to Work Miracles
## with the Limitless Power
## of Psycho-Atomic Energy

# 1

## ULTRA-PSYCHONICS:
### How to Release
### the Surging Power
### of Your "Psychic Atoms"

"It was like the light of a thousand suns!" That was how one man described the explosion of the first atomic bomb three decades ago, and, as much as mere words can, it gives you a faint idea of the awesome power locked in the atom.

Today a new science has been born—an amazing new science that I call ULTRA-PSYCHONICS—and it may well release such mighty power that the famed atomic bomb will look like a firecracker beside it.

ULTRA-PSYCHONICS—the Science of Thought Power—it is here at last!

### The Secret of the Golden Flower

Ultra-Psychonics . . . as new as tomorrow's sunrise . . . yet as old as humanity.

It is based on the teachings of Liu Yen, who first set its principles down in writing in 800 A.D. But it goes back far beyond his time . . . back to the very dawn of civilization. Traditionally, it was known only to kings and wizards . . . and passed on by them only to their oldest sons on their deathbeds.

What is this Secret which has been called the "terrace of life" . . . the "land without boundaries" . . . and the "altar on which consciousness and life are made"? Sometimes it is expressed by a mandala called "The Golden Flower" . . . other times by a strange phrase, "the square inch field of the square foot house."

According to the ancients, the unity of life and consciousness is symbolized by a central white light which dwells in the "square inch" between the eyes. The Tibetan holy book called the *Bardo Thodol* speaks of it thusly:

> Thine own consciousness, shining, void and inseparable from the Great Body of Radiance hath no birth, nor death, and is the Immutable Light.

This deep Truth is not easily perceived by Western man. But its implications are so staggering . . . so filled with promise of a wonderful new life for you . . . that I urge you to make every effort to do so. But first let me explain it to you more clearly:

Just as ordinary matter is made up of little bits of electricity called "atoms"—the human mind is made up of its thoughts. And every thought is made up of what I call PSYCHIC ATOMS!

And even more astounding, this secret was known for centuries—but kept as the private property of the powerful priests, wizards and kings who ruled mankind. Those who tried to reveal it to the common people were put to death in extremely unpleasant ways.

But even the ancients did not understand the full implications of what they had discovered. They knew that these Psychic Atoms could be used to focus an invisible beam of radiance on someone, for example, and turn him into a cringing, obedient slave. They knew that the radiance between their eyes could be expanded into a mighty invisible sphere that would enable them to see beyond locked doors and read the thoughts of others. But they did not understand *why*—and thus their control was never absolute.

It took modern science to discover that the "psychic atom" . . . just like its physical counterpart . . . can be split into even *smaller* particles!

I should qualify the phrase "modern science" by saying that the whole idea of Ultra-Psychonics is my own theory, belief and philosophy. You will not find anything about it in modern scientific journals, although it is based on some of their latest theories.

That is what this book is about. In it, you will discover fantastic secrets of the mind that can open up a great new life for you!

## Inside the Psychic Atom—the Amazing Earth Forces

I am firmly convinced that every "psychic atom" is composed of three—and only three—kinds of particles:

PSYCHONS: particles charged with ESP Force—the secret behind all psychic phenomena such as telepathy, clairvoyance, magic, dowsing, prophecy and the rest of the occult powers.

ULTRONS: particles charged with Hypnotic Force—the secret behind control over others, love and romance, friendship, job advancement and all forms of mental domination.

EGONS: particles charged with Growth Force—the secret behind good health, long life, perfect memory, speed reading, learning ability, "genius" and communication.

More recently, some scientific advances have suggested the possibility of an Anti-Universe. To me, this implies the existence of three "anti-particles": Anti-Psychons, Anti-Ultrons and Anti-Egons. Of these, and their strange powers, more later.

## How to Control the Subpsychic Particles

Now, if these particles simply existed, and could not be used, there would be no point in writing this book. But this is not the case. Based on personal experiences, and the experiences of others whom I have known, I am certain that these thought-particles can be generated, separated and controlled by the power of the human mind!

I have found, for example, that a hypnotic beam of Ultrons can be focussed on someone so that you can ask him for anything—and get it instantly.

And I have found many, many other uses for these amazing forces. That is what this book is about. In it, you will discover a whole new way of living . . . a way based on incredible powers of the mind. These powers can be yours—if you are willing to put in as little as five minutes a day to master them. Here are the details:

## ULTRA-PSYCHONICS: THE MAIN BRANCHES

There are, of course, hundreds of applications of Ultra-Psychonics—applications for every area of living, from growing wealthy fast to adding a score of years to your lifespan. It would literally take a 40-volume encyclopedia to discuss all of them, and perhaps someday this encyclopedia will be written.

But for now, here are the main branches that this book will cover—the most useful, most common applications of this amazing new science:

### Ultra-Hypnology

This is the branch of Ultra-Psychonics that is sometimes called Powerology or Ultra-Doministics. It deals with control, influence and domination over others no matter how strongly they try to oppose you.

Yet, unlike ordinary hypnosis, you do not use any bright objects or swinging pendulums to gain control over others. You use only words—special words that are ultronically "loaded" with power. Once you say these words, you get your way every time.

And unlike ordinary hypnosis, there are no after-effects. People do not resent being "used" by you—they like it. In fact, you stand much higher in their esteem every time you use this wonder-working power on them.

You'll find full details of this startling use of Ultra-Psychonics in Chapter 2.

### Ultra-Pictronics

This branch of Ultra-Psychonics is one of the most popular. When you use it, in effect, you materialize wealth out of thin air. You channel a golden river of riches into your life, start money flowing toward you endlessly and automatically and start living a life of luxury at long last.

It's just like having a Magic Genie who brings you everything you wish for. Yet it's as scientific and dependable as a computer.

In Chapter 3, you're going to discover the secret of Ultra-

Pictronics and see how you can use it to materialize things like a new car, a wonderful new home, money in the bank, a trip to Europe, a color TV, beautiful clothes, money to pay all your bills, even such nonmaterial things as golden opportunities, investment tips, social position and awards and citations.

## Ultra-Mnemonics

Here is a branch of Ultra-Psychonics that many people have been looking for without success for many years—the secret of having a perfect memory, without having to spend endless hours working at it.

It's almost as if your mind were coated with a "memory glue" that makes the facts you want to remember stick to it, until you're ready to call them up. Then they appear in your mind as if they were being projected in giant letters on a movie screen.

You might describe it as energizing a hidden "memory gland" buried deep in your mind—an organ that specializes in remembering, just as your lungs specialize in breathing and your heart specializes in pumping blood. But although it appears to work this way, it is something entirely different. Chapter 4 will explain it, step-by-step.

## Ultra-Geniology

Ever wished you were able to figure faster? Or wanted to read five times as fast as you do now? Or needed to come up with a dozen good ideas in a hurry, when you were under pressure and couldn't even come up with one?

Ultra-Geniology can help you do all this—and more. In effect, it multiplies your brainpower by as much as a factor of 1,000—makes you into a "super-genius" for as long as you like—and turns the most difficult problems facing you into child's play.

Once you finish reading Chapter 5, you're going to be a new person. It's like getting a four-year college education in 10 minutes.

## Ultra-Egonics

You probably recall that the Egon Particles are connected with the growth force. Ultra-Egonics shows you how to concentrate this force and use it for better health, longer life, fast relief from aches and pains all over the body and more vigor and vitality.

For instance, if you're suffering from a backache that's pure torture no matter if you sit, stand or lie down, Ultra-Egonics will help you get rid of it in just two short hours, without using pills, potions, fancy equipment or exercises of any kind.

Or if you're suffering from a nagging headache, and there's no aspirin handy—you can get rid of it in five minutes or less, using one simple Ultra-Egonics technique.

It's all spelled out for you in Chapter 6, and if you're suffering from a painful ailment right now, I suggest you turn right to that chapter and find the help you need.

### Ultra-Astronics

For thousands of years, people have tried to find out about themselves by consulting the stars. The trouble is that most of them used a pseudo-science called "astrology." Now don't get me wrong—there really *is* a science of astrology, and it works. But it's as different from the old-fashioned kind of astrology as night is from day. It's all based on Ultra-Psychonics.

That's why I decided that Chapter 7 should be called "Ultra-Astronics" rather than "Ultra-Astrology." It will tell you some startling things about yourself, about your friends and even about your enemies. You'll gain powerful new insights into the world around you, understand why some people succeed and others fail, why some times are right for you and others are wrong and how to read the real messages displayed on the cosmic billboard in the sky.

"Know Thyself!" said the sage—here's how to do it!

### Ultra-Divination

Divination is just a 10-dollar word for old-fashioned dows-ing—but Ultra-Divination will turn up a lot more for you than just water.

You're going to find out how to make a radically new kind of divining-rod—one that will find all sorts of buried treasures in the earth: gold, diamonds, valuable minerals, oil, even lost objects.

And you're going to see how to use this device—called the Psychonic Radar Locator—without even leaving your home. You can check out areas thousands of miles away, in deserts, on mountain tops, even under water—and get positive results every time.

What's more, this device is completely nonelectric—uses no power source—and can be carried with you anywhere you go. Chapter 8 tells you exactly how to make one, for just a few pennies.

## Ultra-Magic

Magic really works. Not the old-fashioned kind, but the New Magic based on the forces of Ultra-Psychonics. Take a look at Chapter 9 and see for yourself.

Want money to start rolling in right away? Try a "spell" called Money Polarization. Lonely? Get all the friends you want with the Magnetic Friendship Spell. These are just a few. There are spells for attracting good luck, improving your love life, protecting yourself against black magic and witchcraft and a host of others.

You'll also find a way to make an unusual Double-Eagle amulet to ward off harm, a "quickie" amulet you can make with no equipment at all and an exceptionally powerful and long-lasting amulet to protect your home and worldly goods.

Here, too, is the meaning of signs and omens, and a most peculiar invocation that will bring an invisible Psychic Guardian to keep watch over you.

## Ultra-Prognostics

Can you look into the future and know what lies ahead? "Yes!" says the branch of Ultra-Psychonics that I call "Ultra-Prognostics," and it reveals, step-by-step, exactly how to do it.

In other parts of this book, you'll find ways to look ahead in time and get an idea of what is going to happen by means of signs and omens, telepathic dreams and other means. Ultra-Prognostics is an entirely different method. It is as simple as writing your name—and, I believe, just as certain of success.

The secret of Ultra-Prognostics is disclosed in Chapter 10. There, you'll see how you can build an Ultronic Time-Machine for less than a dollar—and use it to get fast, positive answers on forthcoming events.

Whether you're looking for the name of a future lover, a stock that's due to rise, a horse or a number that's going to win or anything else hidden by the veils of Time—you'll find the answer here.

### Ultra-Numerology

The hidden power of numbers is at work in your life right now. Whether you like it or not, everything you do is controlled by a certain series of digits.

Hard to believe? Think about it. To the Government, you are simply a Social Security Number. If your friends want to call you on the phone, they dial a number, not your name. If someone wants to send you a letter, and make sure it gets there, he needs your Zip Code Number—not to mention the numbers on your charge cards that let you buy gasoline, clothing and a thousand other things.

Ultra-Numerology will show you, for the first time, what all these numbers really mean. You'll see how to start using them to your advantage, how to find the master "UP-Number" that controls the others and how to spot favorable people, places and times numerically. See Chapter 11.

### Ultra-Telepathy

Most of us have heard about telepathy for many years—the rare ability to read other people's minds. But if you've ever tried to actually do it, you know that it's a mighty hard thing to do.

The reason for this is that, until now, no one really knew what telepathy was or how it worked. But with the advent of Ultra-Psychonics, telepathy has become hardly more difficult than making a phone call. This new branch of Ultra-Psychonics is called Ultra-Telepathy, and it will help you read the mind of any man or woman you want to, reveal the thoughts of people many miles away, erect an impenetrable "mind shield" to protect your privacy and perform even more astonishing feats.

In Chapter 12, you'll discover the six stages of Ultra-Telepathy, find out how to set up a Telepathic Power Globe that works on psychonic principles, and see how you can explore the far reaches of time and the universe with your newly acquired "talent."

### Ultra-Kinetics

The next step after telepathy is a giant one. From hearing the thoughts of others, you progress to the actual manipulation of solid objects by the power of your mind alone.

Step-by-step you progress from the control of light and delicate objects to bigger and heavier ones, through a startling technique called "Psychonic Tension" which is fully explained in Chapter 13.

Before you know it, you have conscious control of things like dice and roulette wheels, make things fly through the air with the Ultronic Poltergeist method and can even levitate your own body!

As you obtain greater and greater control over your "psychic atoms," other feats become possible: invisibility, astral travel, psychonic possession of other people's bodies and much, much more.

But the best is yet to come!

## Ultra-Sophology

This is the ultimate branch of Ultra-Psychonics—the secret of true and lasting happiness. Here is the long-sought way to the goal of humanity's greatest sages: Cosmic Illumination. Starting from hints given in the little-known *Bardo Thodol,* the Tibetan Book of the Dead, and from ancient Egyptian and Babylonian scrolls, the techniques of Ultra-Sophology have revealed what may be the underlying unity behind all things—the Master Plan of the Universe.

Once you read this chapter, you will know the meaning of Life, discover your place in the Book of Destiny and speak directly to the Cosmic Mind that rules the Universe.

Chapter 14 is the last stage in Ultra-Psychonics. It is the culmination of many long and arduous years of research. Please do not try to read it now—you will not be able to understand it until you have mastered the rest of this book. But once you are ready for it, I think you will find it to be one of the most profound and rewarding experiences in your life.

## HOW TO START DEVELOPING YOUR ULTRA-PSYCHONIC POWERS IN JUST FIVE MINUTES A DAY

Before you turn to Chapter 2 and start applying your new knowledge of the hidden structure of the mind, you will find the following "rituals" helpful in stimulating the flow of the various subpsychic particles within your "psychic atoms":

## How to Stimulate the Psychonic Flow

1. Lie down in a dark, quiet room. Close your eyes and concentrate on blackness, imagining the entire universe to be filled with a dense, black mist.

2. Now imagine a tiny point of glowing yellow light, like a tiny sun, right in the center of your head.

3. Concentrate on the yellow point for five minutes every day, until it shines bright and clear whenever you create it.

This ritual seems simple, but it has just turned on the "Psychon Generator" in your brain under your conscious control, for the first time in your life. The yellow glow you see in your mind's eye is a beam of *psychons*—the fundamental force that controls all psychic phenomena.

## Focussing the Psychon Beam

1. Turn on your Psychon Generator, in a lighted room

2. Imagine the yellow light is flowing out of your eyes, and that your eyes are concentrating the light through their lenses, as the sun is concentrated by a magnifying glass.

3. Focus on an object 6 inches away from your eyes, and imagine that the two beams of light are both concentrated on it in one bright spot.

4. Now focus on an object 1 foot away, then on one 2 feet away, 3 feet away and so on, until you can move the focus of your eyes anywhere within a range of 10 feet or so, with full intensity and power.

This ritual has just generated the Psychonic Laser—a beam that is the basis for many of the key Ultra-Psychonic powers. Practice the ritual for five minutes every day, preferably during the daytime, until you have the Psychonic Laser under complete control.

During these experiments, incidentally, it is not advisable to smoke, drink or eat. Also, no alcoholic beverage should be taken for at least two hours before the ritual is started. If possible, loose fitting clothing should be worn, although it is not vital. All of these rules are aimed at increasing your ability to concentrate without distraction or mental befuddlement. The greater the degree that you observe them, the greater will be your success.

## How to Stimulate the Flow of Ultrons

The ultrons lie at the core of your "psychic atoms." They are more difficult to free than the psychons, but have correspondingly greater penetrating power when you do so. Follow this ritual:

1. Turn on your Psychon Generator.
2. At the center of the yellow sphere of light, imagine there is a tiny reddish-blue dot. This is the nucleus of the "psychic atom"—and is composed of red ultrons and blue egons.
3. Imagine that the yellow ball of light—the psychon beam—is slowly starting to spin around inside your head. Now increase its speed so that it goes faster and faster. Stop for a while if you feel dizzy, but keep practicing until it is spinning at a very high speed. You have just set up a "psychonic cyclotron," and it is weakening the bonds of the central nucleus under your control.
4. As the yellow ball spins faster and faster, you will start to notice little specks of red leaving the center and flying off in all directions. These are ultrons. Speed up the yellow ball until the space it occupies is filled with a bright red glow. You have now generated the Ultron Beam.

Practice this technique for five minutes every day until you can do it automatically, and can generate the Ultron Beam in 30 seconds or less.

## Focussing the Ultron Beam

1. Generate the Ultron Beam.
2. Imagine that its red rays are shooting out of your eyes, as you did when you created the Psychonic Laser.
3. Practice focussing these beams in the same way as the Psychonic Laser beams. This is the Ultronic Laser. Notice how much more powerful and penetrating the beam feels.

## How to Stimulate the Flow of Egons

The third component of the "psychic atom" is quite unlike the other two. It is much heavier than either one, and cannot be focussed into a beam. On the other hand, it is directly connected with your health and vitality, and thus cannot be ignored.

There are several ways to stimulate the egonic flow. Here is one:

1. Place two pans of water on a table in front of you. One pan should contain cold water, the other warm water from the tap. Place one hand in each pan for about three minutes.

2. Generate an Ultronic Beam and focus it on a nearby blank wall. Concentrate on the blue nucleus of the "psychic atom" in the center of your head. Now imagine that there are wires running from your head down each arm. Let the blue power dots from the center of the nucleus start to flow down each arm, into the fingers, and back again, like an electric circuit.

3. Switch hands. Put the hot hand in the cold water and the cold hand in the warm water. You will feel a very strange sensation. This is *egonic flow*. Try to get the "feel" of it. Practice generating it several times until you can do so without using the pans of water.

## Turning on Your Egonic Computer

Once you have control of your egonic flow, there are a wide variety of ways you can use it. For example, try this:

1. Select any two two-digit numbers, such as 43 and 11. Try multiplying them mentally. As you do so, imagine that you are entering them in a tiny computer inside your head—a computer built out of solid egons, and pulsing with blue egonic power. At first, the answer will come very slowly, but it will come.

2. Keep practicing for five minutes every night just before you fall asleep, using the same two numbers. After a few days, you'll find that the answer comes in a flash. Now try two other numbers. This time the answer will come much faster. In a very short time—perhaps two weeks or less—your egonic computer will be in full operation, giving you high-speed answers to any mathematical problem as fast as you need them.

These are just a few of the many rituals you can use to stimulate and develop your ultra-psychonic powers. As you progress, you will discover others. Keep practicing them. Five minutes a day will pay off in tremendous dividends, as you'll soon find out.

One final word. Undoubtedly, some people will ask, "How can you *see* a psychon or an ultron, when you can't see a real atom? Aren't they too small to really be seen?"

They are completely correct. It really is impossible to see these tiny subpsychic particles, any more than you can see an electron or proton. But what you are doing is manipulating them symbolically.

If you look in the back of your radio or TV set, you can't "see" the electricity. But when you turn the set on, you can see various tubes and bulbs light up. If you have a completely transistorized set, of course, you can't see even that much. But you get results. The TV set produces a picture, the radio produces a voice—and you get information and entertainment from someone miles away.

In the same way, when you go through the procedures that have just been explained, you "turn on" your Ultra-Psychonic powers. And although you can't really "see" them, except in your mind's eye, they are just as real and effective as the electricity and radio waves that power your TV and radio.

The main point in trying to visualize them is to give you a focal point to concentrate your psychic energies on. As you've already seen, they really *are* there and they really work.

## WHAT ULTRA-PSYCHONICS CAN DO FOR YOU

In this chapter, you have seen:

- What the "psychic atom" is composed of, and how you can use this knowledge to work a miracle in your life.
- How Ultra-Hypnology can give you power and control over others.
- How Ultra-Pictronics can materialize the things you want.
- How Ultra-Mnemonics can give you a razor-sharp, crystal clear memory.
- How Ultra-Geniology can multiply your mental powers a thousandfold.
- How Ultra-Egonics can improve your health.
- How Ultra-Astronics can reveal new insights about yourself and others.
- How Ultra-Divination can lead you to buried treasures.

- How Ultra-Magic can bring you good luck and protect you from evil psychic forces.
- How Ultra-Prognostics can prophesy the future with unerring accuracy.
- How Ultra-Numerology can reveal the master numbers that rule your life.
- How Ultra-Telepathy can take you into the minds of men and women all over the world.
- How Ultra-Kinetics can give you direct control over matter by the force of your mind alone.
- How Ultra-Sophology can reveal the way to true peace of mind and lasting happiness.
- How you can develop your various Ultra-Psychonic powers with simple rituals that take only five minutes a day.

Now you are ready for the advanced stages of Ultra-Psychonics. Here they come.

# 2

## ULTRA-HYPNOLOGY:
### How to
### Make Others Do
### What You Want

You are about to discover a new and excitingly different way to control and influence other people—a technique called Ultra-Hypnology.

Unlike ordinary hypnosis, which requires privacy, can be used on only one person at a time and does not work at all on many people, Ultra-Hypnology has practically no limitations:

- It works as well on a thousand people as on one.

- It can be used anywhere, day or night, in public or in private, even in front of crowds of people.

- It is completely safe, unlike hypnosis, and has no after-effects.

- It makes you master of any man or woman you choose to use it on, regardless of age, race or creed. It works equally well on an unresponsive lover, an unfriendly neighbor, a hostile crowd, a stubborn child, a tough boss or anyone else whom you want to see things *your* way.

- It turns your enemies into devoted friends, eager to make amends for the way they've treated you before.
- It lets you control, influence and dominate other people without your saying one word to them, in many situations.
- It makes people like and admire you, no matter what you ask them to do. They're only too happy to cooperate.
- It can be used over the phone, by radio, even on television. You can even make tape recordings or write letters that will have the same effect as your being there in person!

"That's what I want," you're probably saying, "but how can I do these things?" You're about to find out!

Carl P. found out. For weeks his neighbors had been "bugging" him in dozens of little ways: cutting his roses off his fence, leaving beer cans in his driveway, letting their dog loose on his lawn, and having parties that lasted until 3 a.m. Then Carl found out about Ultra-Hypnology. He picked up the phone and said one short sentence to his neighbors—a sentence packed with ultronically "loaded" words. It worked an instant miracle!

His neighbors not only cut out all their annoying little tricks, but also went out of their way to be nice to him from then on. They even mowed his lawn for him while he was away on vacation.

### Ultronically "Loaded" Words That Get Results

What were these ultronically "loaded" words that Carl used? I'm going to tell you what they were in a short while. But first, it's important to understand *why* they worked.

They worked because they were aimed at his neighbors' hidden weakness—a desire to have pleasant neighbors. They worked because they were built around the neighbors' *mental stereotypes*—their mental pictures and ideas of what certain groups were like, whether they really were that way or not. They worked because his neighbors had a *will to believe*—a mental force so powerful that once you learn to take advantage of it, you can get anyone to do what you want—and he will jump to it.

All that Carl P. said to his neighbors was, "If you don't stop bothering us, we're going to move out and sell our house to hippies." That was all he had to say. His neighbors, rightly or wrongly, believed that hippies were dirty, smelly people who would ruin the neighborhood and lower the value of their house. It suddenly became the most important thing in the world for them to please Carl P., to make him happy so that he wouldn't move.

"But," you may say, "my neighbors don't mind hippies at all. In fact, they have three of their own."

The point is that there is someone they *do* mind—someone who they can't stand, and shudder at the thought of living next to. It might be someone of a different political party, or religion, or sexual type. It all depends on their mental stereotypes—and you can find out what they are in five minutes, simply by listening to them talk.

It makes no difference to people what their new neighbors would really be like. Their *will to believe* tells them that all "hippies" (or whatever their mental stereotypes are) are dirty, smelly, horrible creatures, and they quickly convince themselves that they must do anything you want to prevent you from leaving.

Words that stimulate mental stereotypes have an ultronic "charge" on them. Some words are more highly charged than others. I'm sure you can think of an insult or two that will get practically anybody fighting mad. On the other hand, some words have practically no charge at all. And some words have a positive charge—tell a woman she's beautiful, and you get an immediate friendly reaction, especially if you're a man she's interested in.

Of course, it's a little more complicated than that. In the example you just saw, the woman might not believe you—she might already be suspicious of you, or have some other reason to doubt your sincerity. Nevertheless, there are ultronically "loaded" words that will get through to anyone. However, these words vary from person to person and it takes some forethought to select the right ones for a particular man or woman. The ultronically "loaded" words that you select must refer to some real quality in a person—for example, some women will respond more favorably to a comment on their choice of clothes, or their cooking ability, or their mental brilliance. A few minutes' preliminary conversation will show you which words to use.

## The Ultronic Vacuum Technique

An easy way to find out enough about a person is through the use of the "ultronic vacuum." This is a technique based on "charged questions." It forces other people to give you helpful information without their being aware of it.

The key to using this technique is to avoid asking questions that can be answered simply by "yes" or "no" or by one or two words.

For example, suppose that you're applying for a job, and you want to get the interviewer feeling friendly toward you.

Ask questions like: "What sort of work will ⸱ be doing?" or "Is there a good chance for advancement in this company?"

These questions immediately convince the interviewer that you're sincerely interested in the job and arouse a favorable response.

Then try to find out something about him personally. Look around his office for clues. "That's a nice looking bowling trophy up on your bookshelf, Mr. Jones. How did you win it?" Other clues might be a photo of his family or of a pet, a school or wedding ring, an amateur painting on the wall or a pin in his lapel.

Avoid asking questions like: "How many paid holidays do we get a year?" or "How long do we get for lunch?". These questions are loaded negatively, and tend to make the interviewer hostile and unfriendly. Needless to say, avoid comments on politics or religion, or anything else that might be controversial.

The key thing to remember here is that everyone has his own limited—and inaccurate—view of the world, and that this world consists of a set of mental stereotypes. This world is as real to your neighbor as your world is to you. He will respond favorably to any words or phrases that fit into his world, and listen to you as long as you don't attack his mental stereotypes. Find out how to adapt your appeals to his world, and he will do whatever you ask.

## 100 KEY ULTRONICALLY "LOADED" WORDS

What sort of words should you use to take fullest advantage of someone else's mental stereotypes? Here are two lists—one of words that have a positive ultronic loading, and the other of words with a negative loading:

| POSITIVELY LOADED WORDS | | NEGATIVELY LOADED WORDS | |
|---|---|---|---|
| admire | kind | abnormal | loafer |
| alert | livewire | bad | miser |
| beautiful | love | bastard | moron |
| brave | loyal | bitch | nag |
| brilliant | neat | bore | nosey |
| careful | nice | brazen | pervert |
| clean | noble | bum | phoney |
| comfortable | pleasant | busybody | pig |

| | | | |
|---|---|---|---|
| considerate | practical | cheap | pushy |
| cosy | pretty | coarse | quitter |
| delightful | reliable | coward | rat |
| energetic | safe | crook | rotten |
| expert | secure | dirty | rude |
| friend | sincere | dull | shiftless |
| generous | smart | dumb | slob |
| genius | steady | faker | sneaky |
| good | strong | fink | spendthrift |
| goodlooking | sweet | fool | stuck-up |
| gorgeous | talented | hussy | stupid |
| handsome | thoughtful | hypocrite | tramp |
| happy | true | idiot | tricky |
| helpful | valuable | inconsiderate | unreliable |
| home | vigor | irresponsible | unscrupulous |
| honest | warmhearted | lazy | weak |
| jolly | wonderful | liar | wishy-washy |

## How to Use Ultronically Loaded Words to Influence Others

Let's suppose that you are having trouble getting one of your children to keep his room neat. Up till now, you've tried threats, promises, bribes, all to no avail.

Now you launch an all-out ultronic campaign. First, you let him overhear you speaking to your spouse: "You know, I think Johnny is starting to become a real man. His room is starting to look much neater."

Next morning, you compliment your son on the way his room looks. "It really is starting to look good in your room," you smile. "I'm very pleased with you."

A few days of this, and the boy starts to react. The ultronically loaded words are delivering a positive charge to his brain cells, right to the Pleasure Center. He likes it. He wants more.

So he starts to make a few small changes in his room. You notice them, and tell him about it. "Your room sure is shaping up," you say. "I guess neatness just runs in the family." That night, you just happen to serve his favorite dessert for dinner. You don't mention it, or connect it in any way. In fact, if your son mentions it, you tell him it's just a coincidence.

Step by step, you continue the campaign. Whenever he makes another major change in his room, he gets praised and something he likes happens. Whenever he starts to slip back into his old sloppy ways, you ignore it—but somehow, that's the night you serve cabbage (or whatever food he isn't too crazy about).

In a few weeks, he's just as neat as the rest of the family—and all it takes to keep him this way is a reinforcement phrase about once a week or so, for a few months. Then his new habit takes hold, and he just keeps on doing it.

You can see how simple and logical this technique is. It has many applications—you can use a variation of it to get a date, put your boss in the mood to give you a raise, get people who work for you to increase their output—the list is endless.

The main thing is to use words from the positively loaded list, and avoid words from the other. You must never appear to be threatening, criticizing or making fun of the other person. You want to project the ultronic image of a friend, not a critic or an enemy. Silently, you are saying to them: "I like you. I've always liked you. I'm glad to see that something good is happening to you."

## ULTRA-HYPNOLOGY WITHOUT WORDS

Is it possible to make other people follow your commands and desires without your having to say a word?

In some cases, startlingly enough, the answer is "Yes!"

For many years now, scientists have been investigating a phenomenon they call "body language." In the beginning, they found that it was possible to read certain subconscious signals by watching people's bodily movements and positions. For example, they found that if a woman sat with her legs crossed, she was broadcasting a signal to every male in the room to "stay away."

Then the study was broadened to include the hand-gestures that many languages use to amplify the meaning of a sentence—as well as gestures common to all languages (if someone draws his forefinger across his throat, he doesn't have to say another word). Communication with animals came under study—the way a dog can respond to his master's gestures and sounds, without being able to understand a word.

Finally, the new science of Ultra-Psychonics became involved, and the techniques were worked out as part of the development of Ultra-Hypnology.

### How a Mugger was Chased Away with Ultronic Gestures

Mabel K., a student of Ultra-Hypnology, was attacked by a

mugger on a street in San Francisco recently. Although there were dozens of people around, no one moved to help her until she tried a certain "ultronic gesture." In a flash, a crowd formed around her, and the mugger was forced to leave without getting anything.

What did she do? She simply put her hand over her heart, wobbled around a bit and let herself fall to the ground as if she were having a heart attack. (She made sure she fell on top of her purse so that the mugger couldn't get it.)

Unlike her cry for help from the mugger, which would have generated a negative ultronic flow in the crowd, since it would have implied danger, her seeming collapse generated a positive flow. People in the crowd immediately thought, "That woman is having a heart attack. She needs help. It's safe to help her. Let's see if I can give her a hand."

Naturally, this technique would not work if you ran into a mugger in a deserted side street. The technique here might be to pretend to be signalling to nearby policemen, as if this were a "stakeout" or decoy situation set up to trap muggers.

However, according to police experts, the worst thing you can do in a mugging situation is to offer resistance, since many muggers are armed and prepared to kill anyone who makes any trouble for them. Ultronically, such resistance generates a powerful negative flow in the mugger's mind, and makes him strike out to defend himself.

## Secrets of Ultronic Eye Command

Another type of powerful ultronic gesture is known as "eye command" or "ultra-vision influence." It is particularly effective where a contest of wills is involved—for example, where someone is trying to hypnotize you, or convince you of something you don't want to be convinced of, or persuade you to do something you don't want to do.

It also works in reverse. In other words, if you want to convince or persuade someone else, you simply use this technique and turn them into willing listeners who *know* that whatever you're telling them is the absolute Truth.

To develop this power, three steps are required:

1. Sit in front of a mirror and practice staring fixedly into your own eyes. Notice how your eyes look when you do this, and try slight variations of expression and position until you feel that you have achieved the most penetrating

look you can generate. Try to fix this "overwhelming gaze" in your memory, so that you can mentally *see* yourself generating it without the mirror.

2. Practice the look on animals. Cats are best. See if you can "stare down" a cat. It will take several minutes of your most concentrated gaze to do this, especially at first. Don't be surprised if the cat seems to win the first few rounds—they're past masters at this. But they just don't have the willpower to outstare you if you really put your mind to it.

3. Practice the look on strangers on various forms of public transport such as buses, trains, subways and planes. Stare steadily at someone sitting opposite you until you force them to turn their head away or look down. You have just mastered your first human subject.

Now, put this technique to work for you. If there is someone you particularly want to convince of something, the time has come. First, work out a plan of attack. You need three or four persuasive arguments. Write them down ten times each on a sheet of paper, to help you commit them to memory. Then, engage the person you want to convince in an ordinary conversation. Focus the ultron beams coming out of your eyes on him with the Ultronic Eye Command technique you've just mastered. Now, start working your persuasive arguments into the conversation. Keep them as positive as possible, using the ultronic "loaded" word technique you learned earlier.

In just a few minutes, you'll find that the other person is agreeing with you at long last. His or her resistance has been completely demolished by this "talking eye" technique!

### How to Make Ultronic Gestures

An ultronic gesture should never be made coldly and mechanically. Instead, it should start deep inside you, at the center of your body, and flow out of it. A hand gesture, for example, should flow out of your fingertips, ultronically charged with a strong emotion.

If it is used in conjunction with "loaded" words and phrases, the gesture should be timed so that it coincides with them, or even precedes them slightly. It should never follow them—late timing is entirely ineffective, and may even make people laugh at you.

The gesture should also be suited to the size of the audience. A finger may be enough to get something across to one or two people; whereas, a full, sweeping arm-and-hand gesture would be required for a larger group.

It is vital that you never indicate that you are aware of your own gestures, as this makes them seem mechanical and robs them of their effectiveness. They must seem to be completely spontaneous.

Another point is to keep things moving along. A moving object is infinitely more attention-compelling than one that remains still. Thus, for example, if a rather seedy-looking beggar came to your door for a handout, and you wanted to get rid of him fast, you might try simply pointing at him, moving your arm with your index finger outstretched, from the center of your chest to your side, with a steady, rapid motion. You would use your right or left hand for this, depending on which way you wanted him to go to get off your property. Without saying a word, you've told him, "Get lost, you bum!"

## ULTRONIC SUGGESTION:
## THE KEY TO POWER OVER PEOPLE

Ultronic Suggestion is the heart of Ultra-Hypnology—it produces the effects of hypnosis without using any form of hypnotism whatsoever.

You have been exposed to this type of suggestion all your life. You are constantly being bombarded with ads, political speeches and other kinds of messages—all carefully aimed at making you do something you may not want to do.

Now, for the first time, you are going to discover the laws that rule this type of verbal mind-control—and see how you can amplify and increase their effectiveness with the techniques of Ultra-Hypnology.

### The Eight Main Techniques of Ultronic Suggestion

There are eight different ways to use Ultronic Suggestion— eight ways of getting people to do what you want, and making them think that it's their own idea:

### 1. Psychosomatic Suggestion

This is aimed directly at the link between mind and body.

For example, if you tell someone day after day that he isn't looking well, eventually he will become sick. Perhaps you have seen something similar, where a group of people keep telling a person who's a little under the weather that he looks "terrible." By the end of the day, he's really ill. Another example of this would be ads that invent imaginary diseases, such as "B.O." or "halitosis"—and then present their product as the solution to it.

### 2. Archetype Suggestion

An archetype is a prestige figure. He may come across as the Wise Old Man, or the All-Powerful King, or the Great Expert. By attributing a statement to him, you invoke his special authority and arouse a submissive attitude.

You see this principle in action all around you. Baseball and football stars endorse shaving cream on TV. Politicians claim they are following the paths laid out by former great Presidents.

This type of suggestion is very strong. Everyone wants to follow in the footsteps of a great leader. But the archetype must be carefully selected, since different leaders appeal to different people. The Ultronic Vacuum technique should be used to draw out the subject first, and find out exactly whom he admires and respects.

### 3. Direct Suggestion

In this type of suggestion, you come right to the point. You tell your listener exactly what you want him to do, using ultronically "loaded" words so that the idea sounds appealing.

For example, a salesman might say, "Write your name here as you want it to appear on your deed," although what he really is saying is, "Sign the contract."

Direct suggestion can be very successful, provided you push the right "psychic buttons" in the other person's mind. However, it works best from a higher authority level to a lower one. Otherwise, the reaction it creates may be, "Who are *you* to tell *me* what to do?"

### 4. Indirect Suggestion

This is one of the subtlest and most effective forms of suggestion known, since it makes the subject think that the suggestion he has received is really his own idea.

This technique was used by both sides in the 1972 election campaign very effectively. In TV ads, the sponsoring party would quote a statement that their opponent had made a number of years before that was now embarrassing to him: "Those who can't end the war should be defeated at the polls" or "Everyone in the country should get 1,000 dollars a year from the Government"— and let the listeners draw their own conclusions.

### 5. Positive Suggestion

This type of suggestion stresses the affirmative. All words and phrases with negative images are eliminated. For example, if you want a child to avoid bothering a pet dog, you would say, "Henry, come over and watch this great new TV show," rather than "Henry, don't bother the dog. Come over here and watch TV instead." In the second case, you have planted the seeds for trouble, by mentioning a competing negative idea that may eventually prove too attractive to resist.

### 6. Negative Suggestion

Obviously, the negative idea may deliberately be presented this way. For example, if you wanted someone to open a package, you might deliberately mark it, "Do not open till Xmas," knowing that they simply can't resist doing it.

It is widely used in politics to get people to vote *against* the opponent rather than *for* the candidate.

### 7. Reverse Suggestion

This works like a charm on people who resist all other types of suggestion, the "Mary, Mary, quite contrary" type.

I met a Ph.D. once who told me that the only reason he had entered college at all was because one of his high school teachers told him that he "wasn't college material." To prove her wrong, he went on to graduate at the top of his high school class, and took many honors in college.

It's very effective on children: "Donnie, you aren't big enough to help me rake up the leaves" or "Sally, you're not old enough to wash the dishes yet." Before you know it, little Donnie and Sally are being extra good for the privilege of helping you with the household chores!

### 8. Auto-Suggestion

This type of suggestion works on *you*—it convinces you that you can and will do things you previously believed to be impossible.

David S., a young salesman just starting out on a new job, found that he lacked the courage and self-confidence to really perform effectively. To build himself up, he decided to apply this Ultra-Hypnology technique by making up about a dozen little cards that said simply "I am the world's greatest salesman." He stuck them up all over his house: over his shaving mirror, on his dresser, even on the breakfast table. He taped one to the visor of his car, and even put up a few at work. The older men laughed at him—but they stopped laughing in six weeks when he became the top salesman in the company, and a year later became sales manager.

## CONTROLLING GROUPS OF PEOPLE WITH THE ULTRONIC "ZONE OF INFLUENCE"

All of the above techniques can be used with equal effect on individuals and groups. You can use them to sway and influence anyone. But if you're interested in controlling large groups of people, there are some additional Ultra-Hypnology techniques that are extremely effective. They work by creating an ultronic "Zone of Influence."

### Ultra-Atmospherics

This technique involves "setting the stage" for your message. For example, a torchlight parade arouses man's primitive emotions. Make a speech at night with the light provided only by torches or a fire, and you magnify your impact by a factor of 1,000 or more.

Symbols are all important. The audience should be prepared for them in advance, and they should be prominently displayed. Other symbols that offer opposing or distracting ideas must be removed.

Music, too, can set the stage. It should be suited to the occasion—patriotic songs for political meetings, organ music for a religious gathering and so on.

Some of these techniques have been used with tremendous effectiveness all through history. Kings, emperors, dictators, presidents, religious leaders have all used them to rise to power and to persuade millions to follow their cause.

But the technique can be used on a smaller scale with similar effectiveness. A salesman who sells to the rich can get his message across with much greater effect in a plush hotel suite. An executive can convey an image of power to his subordinates by the size and furnishings of his office. And even a pushcart peddler can convey the low price of his merchandise by using crude hand-lettered signs and dressing very shabbily. There are "blind" beggars in the streets of our major cities who ride to their "work" in Cadillacs.

## Ultra-Togetherness

A "polarized" audience is the goal of this technique—a technique that welds a crowd into a single unit, all enthusiastically receptive to the message of the speaker.

The speaker says "we"—never "you" or "I"—and he concentrates on melting individual differences between the members of his audience until they are ripe for his message.

The technique is amplified outside the meeting place by special recognition signals: special handshakes, insignia, greeting phrases. Special bonuses and rewards, perhaps, might be given for recruiting new members. The emphasis is on *growth*.

That, of course, is the ultimate expression of this technique. On a smaller scale, group unity can be forged at meetings by such relatively simple devices as asking for a show of hands on a question that will generate a 95% or better "yes" response. Or a group can be asked to sing a club song, a school anthem or even a hymn. It all depends on the group, and what your ultimate goal for them is.

## The Common Ultronic Bond

This technique was used effectively in World War II by Winston Churchill to hold the British nation together, by Franklin Delano Roosevelt to unite the nation in the face of the Great Depression and by other leaders all through history to minimize disagreements and get others to follow them. You will even find it in the Bible.

What you need here is a series of statements that your audience will agree with. "You all know that . . . " is the way these statements are usually phrased, and the longer the string of them, the better. Toward the end, you can slip in a few statements that perhaps everyone might not have agreed with when your talk started—but in the context of your speech, in the climate of agreement you have "engineered," the statements seem perfectly reasonable and unarguable.

Another variation of this technique is the "just plain folks" approach. You've seen politicians use this before elections: kissing babies, eating various ethnic foods, wearing hard hats or Indian war bonnets. You may remember some years back one politician made a big thing out of having a hole in his shoe, and another tried to stress that his wife wore only cloth coats and not fur ones.

### Ultronic Rationalization

This is a valuable shortcut you can use when you run across people who are favorable to your ideas or personality. You simply provide them with some seemingly logical reasons for doing what you want them to. People don't like to appear irrational to themselves, or to others—it sets up a negative ultronic charge in their mind that disturbs them. The logical "reasons" you provide them with carry a positive ultronic charge which cancels this out.

For example, few people will admit buying a new car because they like the way it looks. They're much happier if they can say something like, "Not only is it a great-looking car, but it has all the latest safety devices." Or, " . . . it gets 25 miles to the gallon."

You can study this technique easily by noting ads for products which are practically identical with their competitors, such as soap, aspirin, cigarettes and breakfast cereals.

### Ultronic Repetition

The more frequently you present a suggestion, the stronger it becomes. An ultronic charge builds up on it that literally blasts through any obstacle or objection.

Hard to believe? Here's proof: In 1943, Kate Smith spoke on CBS radio for one and two minutes at repeated intervals for 18 hours, urging people to buy U.S. War Bonds. She varied her message many ways, but kept repeating one slogan over and over, "Will you buy a bond?" When listeners were queried afterwards, that slogan was the only thing many of them could remember about her "ads." Was it effective? Well, on that one day Kate Smith sold *39 million dollars* worth of bonds.

### Ultronic Targeting

This technique consists of finding a "scapegoat" to blame

existing problems on. By directing people's stored-up ultronic energies at such a target, the impression is created of actually having a solution to the problems, although what is actually involved is simply a focussing of these energies upon a convenient, external target.

This technique was widely employed in the Presidential election campaign of 1972, by both major parties. It is a dangerous technique to use against an opponent who can fight back with the same weapons, as the loser found out. Furthermore, the technique has the potential to create a great deal of trouble and misery if the target groups or person is not able to put up a defense. The technique was used by the ancient Romans against the early Christians, and in more recent times by the Nazis, the Russians and the Red Chinese against various groups. It was horribly effective.

## Ultronic Brainwashing

This is a fairly new technique, developed out of Pavlov's experiments with dogs. Basically, it consists of putting people through the three stages of ultronic exhaustion:

*Stage 1*—The people are so tired that a loud noise or its equivalent is needed to get their attention. Things that should be important to them are overlooked or ignored.

*Stage 2*—In the next stage, they become enormously aware of small changes around them, and ignore the things that caught their attention in Stage 1.

*Stage 3*—In the final stage of ultronic exhaustion, a complete turnabout takes place. People suddenly agree to things that they formerly refused to accept. They sign anything, give you any information you want and become your loyal supporters. What is more, this change is *permanent*—the new mental outlook persists even after the exhaustion is relieved.

## Other Techniques

The "Big Lie" technique, backed up with "experts," sweeping claims and undocumented statistics, can be very effective, particularly if the actual facts are hard to determine.

"Psychological warfare" depends on surprise attacks, threats and seemingly irrational moves to throw the opposition off-balance.

"Word manipulations" consist of finding the right words to describe your cause or to attack someone else's. Retreat becomes a "strategic withdrawal," the poor become the "disadvantaged" and mourning becomes "grief therapy." Call a law the "Right to Work Law" and it attracts wide support, even though its opponents protest in vain that its main purpose is "union-busting." Shakespeare said that "a rose by any name would smell as sweet"—this may be true, but if you call it a stinkweed, not too many people are going to take a sniff.

### How Alan J. Used Ultra-Hypnology to Win a Promotion

Alan J. was about ready to quit his job, when he heard of Ultra-Hypnology. For years, the other people in the office had been making fun of him, saying things about him to the boss behind his back and snubbing him in dozens of different ways.

He decided to try three of the Ultra-Suggestion techniques. First, he built up his own self-image using Auto-Suggestion, simply by carrying a card in his pocket that said "I am top man in the office." He looked at it several times a day and mentally repeated it every chance he got.

Then he tried Indirect Suggestion. He pretended to be getting phone calls from another company, and let his boss overhear conversations like: "Well, Head File Clerk is a nice title, but the job pays only a couple thousand more. I have some good pension benefits where I am now. I'll think it over and let you know."

Finally, he tried Reverse Suggestion. "Mr. Jenkins," he said to his boss, "I have the feeling that some people here want me to leave. How do *you* feel about it?"

His boss assured him that he didn't want him to leave at all, and in fact was in line for a promotion and a raise in the near future. A few weeks later, this all came true!

### How Susan H. Became President of Her Club

Susan H. is convinced that Ultra-Suggestion really works. Shortly before her club held its annual election for president, she used Negative Suggestion on the woman who held the office. She kept stressing the enormous amount of work the woman had to do as president, and how little help and appreciation she got. When the woman was renominated for president, she declined. To her great surprise, Susan was nominated, accepted the nomination and was elected president that very day!

## How to Create an Ultronic "Zone of Influence"

Any, or all of these techniques can be used to create an ultronic "Zone of Influence" for controlling groups of people. You can use them at home, at work, in your social life, in community affairs and in many other situations.

The first step in establishing such a "Zone of Influence" is to sit down with a pencil and paper, and analyze the situation:

- How many people are there in the group you want to control?

- How much money (if any) do you have to spend on this?

- Which techniques can be applied to this problem?

After you have decided which ones you want to use, the next step is to assemble whatever materials you may need.

Then, try the techniques by yourself in a "dry run" or rehearsal of what you plan to do. Make sure you have everything under control.

Next, try the techniques out on the group you want to dominate. Watch for "feedback"—see how the group reacts as you introduce each new aspect. You may want to drop some angles, and concentrate more on others.

Finally, when you have everything going perfectly, carry each technique to completion. You have now established an ultronic "Zone of Influence" over the group, and it is yours to command!

## How to Protect Yourself from Outside "Zones of Influence"

By now, you've probably recognized a number of these techniques that other people have used or are trying to use on you.

Perhaps your boss has tried to use "brainwashing" on you by waiting till you're tired at the end of the day, and then suggesting that you take work home.

Perhaps a neighbor has tried to stir you up against new people moving into the neighborhood.

Perhaps a salesman has tried to "high-pressure" you into buying something you don't want.

Perhaps a politician you don't like is trying to get you to vote for him.

What can you do? The first step is to let the other person talk enough so that you can see which of the methods you've just read about is being used on you.

Then, figure out his true purpose. What is he *really* trying to get you to do?

Stopping him is simple. In effect, you fight fire with fire. Simply map out your own campaign, using the techniques you've just learned, and use it on him.

For example, suppose your neighbor is trying to get you to sign a petition you don't want to sign. You tell him that you can't sign just then, but will sign later that day. Then you "fake" your own petition, on something you know he's opposed to. When you see him later, you tell him, "Of course, I'll sign your petition—if you'll sign mine." Naturally, he refuses. "I can't sign that," he says, "I don't agree with it." "Well," you smile, "I guess I can't sign yours either." Thus, you avoid signing, and yet avoid having an unpleasant confrontation with him. In fact, he's likely to admire you.

## WHAT ULTRA-HYPNOLOGY CAN DO FOR YOU

Ultra-Hypnology gives you power over others without using hypnosis or hypnotic devices. It uses ultronically "loaded" words to control and direct the actions and thoughts of others. In this chapter, you've seen:

- How to make your neighbors cut out their irritating little tricks and stop "bugging" you.
- How to get an immediate friendly reaction from any man or woman.
- How to discover a person's mental stereotypes through the use of the "ultronic vacuum."
- How to make a favorable impression on a job interviewer.
- How to use 100 key ultronically "loaded" words.
- How to get a child to straighten up his room and keep it neat.
- How to control other people without saying a word by means of ultronically "loaded" gestures.

- How to handle a mugger.

- How to use ultronic eye command to convince others that your ideas are right.

- How to get rid of beggars and panhandlers without speaking to them.

- How to use the eight main types of ultronic suggestion to dominate others.

- How to control groups of people by setting up ultronic "zones of influence."

- How to protect yourself from "zones of influence" set up by others.

Of course, this is only the barest outline of the many benefits you can derive from Ultra-Hypnology. Each technique should be practiced for at least five minutes a day until it is mastered. As your control over others is developed and perfected, you will notice more and more changes in your life. For the first time, things will start to go the way you want them to. You will win raises, promotions, make scores of new friends and have a much happier and pleasanter home and social life.

And that's just the beginning!

# 3

## ULTRA-PICTRONICS:
### How to
### Materialize the Riches
### You Desire

A short time from now, you're going to turn on your hidden money-making powers full blast . . . and then watch in amazement as more money comes rolling in than you've ever seen in your life!

Using the techniques of the incredible new science of Ultra-Pictronics, you're going to start to make your money supply grow as it has never grown before . . . quickly running up even the smallest amounts into thousands of dollars . . . and keeping it growing month after month, year after year, endlessly and automatically.

In effect, it's like having your own "Money Fountain," spraying coins and bills, diamonds and jewels and torrents of golden riches into the air. All you have to do is reach out and grab some, and you have . . .

- money to buy a big, expensive new home in the best part of town!
- money to wipe out all the debts you have, with one glorious payment that gets rid of them forever!

- money to purchase a sparkling new automobile—whether you want a Cadillac, a Chrysler Imperial, a Rolls-Royce or any other kind of car!
- money in your bank account, steadily increasing at the top interest rates in the country!
- money for a giant wardrobe of the latest, most stylish clothes!
- money to travel anywhere in the world, first class—on the best airplanes, luxury liners and super-trains!
- money to educate your children at the finest colleges and universities in the country!

Best of all, it makes absolutely no difference whether you "need" the money or not ... whether you want money for "worthwhile" purposes ... or just for fun. Ultra-Pictronics is going to bring you all the money you've ever dreamed about—and then some!

Step-by-step, Ultra-Pictronics is going to help you get things like a brand new car, a big raise and promotion on your job, a better and more luxurious place to live, a new color TV set, new and satisfying romance, the finest and most expensive cuts of meat on your table and much, much more.

Ultra-Pictronics is the answer you've been looking for all your life. It will help you charge your money goals with throbbing ultronic power, and make their achievement seem simple and natural. Without Ultra-Pictronics, these goals are just a hollow shell ... with it, you're off like a rocket to the moon!

## Amazing Techniques Work Miracles Overnight

In the next few pages, the techniques of Ultra-Pictronics are going to be revealed to you. You're going to see how techniques like "ultra-glyphics," "psychonic repetology," "verbal invocation," "graphic invocation," "reverse money-flow" and "ultronic multiplication" can work miracles in your life—actually overnight in many cases.

Here are the money secrets that the rich won't tell—the magic talismans that turn ordinary matter, in effect, into piles of shining gold. For centuries the few that accidentally discovered these techniques grew rich beyond the dreams of avarice. Yet even they did not know *why* these techniques worked—and they could not apply them scientifically. Now ordinary men and women can use these techniques to duplicate the fortunes of these early wealth-kings—and go far beyond them. You are about to discover the Ultra-Pictronic laws that bring abundance—laws that you can use quickly and easily to reap a golden harvest of wealth.

## THE ULTRA-PICTRONIC ROAD TO RICHES

### How Harold B. Got a New Car

Harold B.'s friends and neighbors were shocked a few months ago when they saw him driving around in a brand new Cadillac.

"How can he afford it?" they keep asking each other. "He's just barely keeping his head above water with that low paying job of his."

What they didn't know—and what would have surprised them even more—was that Harold had bought the car outright, and didn't owe a penny on it!

How did he do it? Harold B. got his new Cadillac with the help of a remarkable technique called "ultra-glyphics"—a technique that lets you simply "will" things into existence—creating them, in effect, out of thin air.

The process was simple. Every night, after work, Harold spent a few minutes setting up a scrapbook in which he collected everything he could find about Cadillacs. He cut ads out of newspapers and magazines, got dealer literature from Cadillac showrooms and even took photos of them on the street. Soon he became an expert on every model, style and accessory that Cadillac put out. And he kept tabs on prices by following ads for new and used Cadillacs closely in his local paper.

He knew so much, in fact, that one of the dealers whose showroom he visited was impressed. He offered Harold a part-time job evenings and weekends as a salesman. Harold took the job eagerly—and because he knew the car backwards and forwards, he quickly outsold most of the other salesmen. In a few months, he had more than enough money to buy the exact Cadillac he wanted—and what made it even better was that he got it at a big discount.

That is the essence of the ultra-glyphics technique. First, you set up a scrapbook, and fill it with every fact, figure and picture you can find of the thing you want.

Then you study all the price angles until you're aware of every possible price break. Sometimes you can work for the thing you want, like Harold. Sometimes you will discover a special discount store or an auction house where you can pick up what you want for a song. And sometimes, to your delight, you will find that the money you need just comes to you out of the blue!

The simple act of concentrating your desires on one object works like a "money magnet" to bring in the cash you need.

## The Secret of Getting a Pay Raise When You Want It

Of course, sometimes the thing you want is not something physical. Perhaps you want a promotion, a pay raise or a particular job.

There's another Ultra-Pictronic way to get these things. It's called "psychonic repetology"—and it can work like a charm for you. The basic technique is simple—you take several sheets of paper and a pen, and write the thing you want over and over—until you have written it exactly 666 times. This magic number "unlocks" the brain cells and channels your psychonic flow into a roaring torrent of energy that brings you the result you want.

Take Richard L., for example. He could barely scrape along on $10,000 a year, due to his large family. He needed a pay raise badly, but his boss just kept stalling him.

Then he tried psychonic repetology—writing down over and over, "I must have a raise," until he had written it the required number of times.

The next day he walked right into the boss' office, looked him straight in the eye and told him he *had* to give him a raise. The confrontation paid off! His boss simply couldn't say "no."

In fact, when he saw how determined Richard L. was, he not only knuckled under, but also gave an even bigger raise than Richard had hoped for!

You, too, can use this technique successfully. All that's required is that you keep thinking about what you want as you write it down. It should never become mechanical. For example, *each time* you write down, "I must have a raise," you should think about why you must have it and what you need it for.

"How does this method really work?" you may ask. According to my Ultra-Psychonic research, it works by setting up a circular path in your mind similar to that in a cyclotron. Just as the electronic particles in a cyclotron are whipped around faster and faster until they burst forth with a colossal bolt of power, so, too, the ultrons in your mind are accelerated to fantastic strengths.

When Richard L. had his showdown with his boss, it was as if a "Command Ray" flashed from his eyes—a steady, unwavering glare that melted his boss' resistance, just as the hot July sun melts an ice cube.

### How Alice C. Got a Better Place to Live

Suppose the thing you want is not easy to achieve through either of the preceding two methods. Alice C., for example, felt she was paying too much money for a small and uncomfortable apartment in a poor part of town. Was there a way Ultra-Pictronics could help her?

There certainly was—an unusual technique called "verbal invocation." Once Alice learned this method, she put it to work for her immediately. What she did was to make sure that she mentioned her need for an apartment to everyone she met, every time she spoke to them. It made no difference whether they were relatives, friends, neighbors, chance acquaintances, co-workers, mailmen, store clerks, even perfect strangers. Over and over, in every conversation, she kept telling these people about her urgent need for a bigger and better apartment.

It paid off sooner than she had ever dared to dream! Within two weeks, her grocer tipped her off to a vacancy that was exactly what she was looking for. She rushed right over and signed the lease at a rent that was actually less than what she was paying before, and got two extra rooms in the bargain!

This technique is remarkably easy to use, especially if you come in contact with a lot of people every day. After a few days, it's just as if you were broadcasting a psychic television commercial—and, in a sense, you are. Before you know it, you've enlisted a large army of unpaid volunteers to help you—and, as the word spreads from one person to another, it even includes people you've never met and don't know at all!

You can use this terrific technique at home, on the job, on buses and trains, even at parties. And as you can see, you really do very little—most of the work is done by other people.

### Power from "Charged" Letters

A powerful variation of the "verbal invocation" technique is called "graphic invocation." To use this method, you write a special kind of letter to many different people, telling them exactly what you want. You write to friends and relatives, of course, but also to rich people, executives in big companies, even government officials.

Edith L., for example, badly wanted a color TV set, but couldn't afford it on her small Social Security income. Using this technique, she wrote to her friends and relatives all over the country, and to heads of all the big TV manufacturing companies. Within a few days, to her great surprise, not only was she offered several used color TV sets, but two of the companies even offered her brand-new ones for about a quarter of what a set would have cost her in a store!

The great thing about this technique is that you can do it right from your own home, without having to make much effort. For example, once you work out a letter to one relative or one type of manufacturer, you can use the same wording over and over with just minor variations. Another advantage is its low cost—all you need are a few sheets of paper, some envelopes and a few stamps. Edith L. invested less than 5 dollars and saved hundreds of dollars this way.

## The Secret That Makes This Technique Work Miracles

Of course, just writing ordinary letters will work to some extent for you—but there's a better way. All you need do is apply the techniques of ultra-psychonic power you've already heard about. For instance, in this case, after you seal and stamp each letter, you simply hold it against your forehead for a few seconds and project a beam of ultrons into the paper. Thus, your desires will impregnate the letter and turn it into an instrument of many times the power it had before.

Once you've mastered this simple technique, you can use it for many other things besides getting TV sets, of course. You can write for—and get—special deals on travel and vacations—reductions on college tuitions—big discounts on clothing—and even money itself, all just for the asking. It's just like standing under your own "Money Fountain" and having torrents of golden riches rain down on you!

## Reverse Money-Flow Brings You Cash Fast—Fast—Fast!

The next Ultra-Pictronic wealth secret you're going to discover is called "reverse money-flow"—and it's a shocker.

How would you like to spend 10 dollars—and find yourself with the same money back in your pocket the very next day? Or mail a check off to pay your bills, and find at the end of the month that the cash is still in your bank account?

These are just two ways that reverse money-flow keeps money coming back to you, to be used over and over.

## How Tom M. Got the Boat of His Dreams—Free!

Reverse money-flow worked wonders for Tom M., a young office worker. For many years he had wanted a 22-foot sailboat, but just couldn't manage to put the money aside from his small salary.

Finally, he saved up enough to make a down-payment on one. The very next day, he heard about reverse money-flow and decided to give it a try. To his complete surprise, a week later he got a letter from an old friend of his offering him the same kind of boat absolutely free.

"I know I should charge you money for it," his friend wrote, "but for some strange reason, I just don't feel I should."

Tom accepted the boat with pleasure—and cancelled his order. In a few weeks, like clockwork, his down-payment money flowed back into his account.

## Let Reverse Money-Flow Bring Back Every Dollar You Spend!

Why did the money come back to Tom? Was it just coincidence—or something more? Try it yourself and see. Here's all you have to do:

1. Every night, just before you go to sleep, put your financial papers under your pillow. By financial papers, I mean things like cash in your wallet, credit cards, check books, bank books, uncashed checks from others (for instance, your paycheck or Social Security check) and all your bills that are still unpaid.

2. Just before you fall asleep, turn on your Psychon Generator (as explained in Chapter 1) and focus the psychic laser beam on the financial papers under your pillow.

3. Sing the following "money chant" to the tune of "My Bonnie Lies Over the Ocean":

> My money lies under my pillow
> My money is right here with me

> No matter what I spend tomorrow
> Bring back my money to me.
> Bring back—bring back—
> Yes, bring back my money to me!

You may feel a little silly at first, when you do this. But in a few days, when the money starts rolling back in, you'll feel quite differently.

## How to Become an "Instant Millionaire"

And now we come to perhaps the greatest money-secret of them all—"ultronic multiplication"—the secret that can make you a millionaire virtually overnight.

The technique works by shifting the Laws of Chance in your favor. Once you start to use it, you win over and over at cards, on the horses, in lotteries and contests and anywhere else Lady Luck is operating. Of course, the game has to be honest—even Ultronic Multiplication can't beat a marked deck or loaded dice. But if it is, you're going to win high, wide and handsome!

Earl B. is the living proof of that. Until he learned the secret of Ultronic Multiplication, he was living from hand to mouth, gambling his money away as fast as he could earn it.

Overnight, the secret of Ultronic Multiplication changed his life. From a born loser, he became a born winner. Before he knew it, all his gambling debts were paid off, and the money started to flow in faster than he had ever dreamed it could. Today, he owns his own casino in Las Vegas, and is richer than many millionaires whose names you see in the papers all the time.

## How to Control the Laws of Chance

How many times have you noticed that you have "good days" and "bad days"? There are days when everything you touch turns to gold, and days when you just can't seem to win, no matter how hard you try.

If there was only some way you could be sure—in advance—as to the kind of luck you were going to have, think of what a difference it would make!

You would know, for example, whether or not to go into a card game . . . how much you ought to bet . . . and when to stop.

Or you might be more interested in whether or not to bet on a particular race . . . or which day was the best to buy your lottery ticket.

Ultronic Multiplication solves all these problems for you with one simple action. It's called "luctronics"—and it points the way for you just as a road map points out the right road to wherever you want to go.

Here's how it works: Just before you get ready to join the game, or buy your lottery ticket, or whatever else is involved, you "test" your luck. You take a special penny—it must be a new one of the current year—and wash it carefully with soap and water, saying the following money-chant:

> One for the money
> Seven for the show
> Show me the answer—
> Which way to go?

Then you dry the penny carefully, and toss it exactly seven times, making a note of how many heads and tails come up. Depending on the results, here's your plan of action:

| | |
|---|---|
| SEVEN HEADS | . . . your luck is at its peak |
| SIX HEADS | . . . your luck is very strong |
| FIVE HEADS | . . . your luck is barely operating |
| FOUR HEADS | . . . your luck is just average |
| THREE HEADS | . . . your luck is weak |
| TWO HEADS | . . . your luck is very weak |
| ONE HEAD | . . . your luck is strongly against you |
| NO HEADS | . . . your luck is at rock bottom |

As you can see, the Luctronic Test is completely scientific and positive. It gives you clearcut answers that tell you exactly what to do.

If, for example, you toss seven heads just before entering a poker game, you know that you're going to win—and you can bet accordingly.

On the other hand, if you get four heads or less on the day you're thinking of buying a lottery ticket, it's obviously better not to do it and to wait for a more favorable day.

If you toss five heads just before a race, then you should obviously keep down the size of your bet.

There is one slight danger with this method that should be mentioned: If someone else is using the same technique, it may cancel yours out, or even overcome it. If you have any inkling that this might be the case, drop out immediately.

In order to get the full benefit out of the Luctronic Test, you should combine it with the other techniques of Ultronic Multiplication. For example, once you know that the day is going to be a good one for you, you can multiply its favorable aspects by taking certain actions:

1. *Ultra-Psychonic Exercises*—Run through the creation of the Psychon Beam, the Psychic Laser, the Ultron Beam, the Ultronic Laser and the Egonic Computer. These exercises hone your mind to a fine edge, and give you that "something extra" that can make the difference between just winning—and winning *big!*

2. If you are buying a lottery ticket, put it in a "lottery nest." This is a special envelope filled with clippings from your daily paper about the people who have won the previous lotteries. Each clipping radiates beneficial vibrations that will help to increase your chance of winning.

3. If you are going to play cards, about an hour or two before the game, take a fresh pack and hold each card up to your forehead and project a beam of psychons through it. This helps to sensitize your mind, so that you can get telepathic impulses from the other players while the game is in progress. When conditions are right, you can practically know every card they hold in their hands.

4. If you are watching a race, you can give your horse extra energy by standing on one foot and projecting a Psychic Laser at his hindquarters. This is called the "Astral Spur" technique, and works by disrupting your egonic flow through unbalancing your body. The smooth output of your Psychic Laser is twisted by this, and its beam becomes much rougher and more abrasive. If you cannot be at the race in person, somewhat the same effect can be attained by projecting a twisted Psychic Laser beam at the horse's name printed in your newspaper or racing form. However, the effect is much weaker.

5. Dice can also be controlled with a twisted Psychic Laser, but control is very delicate and should be practiced privately for a few hours each day until you master it.

## Why Ultronic Multiplication Must Work for You

There should be no doubt in your mind that Ultronic

Multiplication is going to work for you. Why? Because it has worked for scores of men and women in all walks of life. It made no difference if they had previously been unlucky or not, or whether they were rich or poor, old or young. Ultronic Multiplication worked like a charm every time.

Here are some of the people it has helped:

Ted M. of Chicago was about to be evicted by his landlord for nonpayment of rent. Once he learned this technique, he went downtown on the right day and won five times as much money as he needed in just one hour with the dice!

Larry S. had expensive tastes that his low salary as an office worker just couldn't seem to satisfy. He tried Ultronic Multiplication in a few friendly lunchtime poker games, and found he was able to more than double his salary week after week!

Arthur C. liked to play the ponies, but he was a steady loser until he heard about Ultronic Multiplication. Now he only goes to the track once or twice a week—but he does so well that he no longer has to work for a living. Instead of him supporting the horses, the horses are now supporting him!

Louise F. could barely scrape along on her late husband's Social Security money till she tried Ultronic Multiplication. Now she's already won the state lottery twice, and is set for life!

Robert M., an underpaid bookkeeper with a large family, could hardly afford to feed them until Ultronic Multiplication lent a hand. Not a gambling man, Robert M. tried this amazing technique on the stock market—and found, to his astonishment, that it worked even better there than on games of chance. He ran the Luctronic Test on each stock he was thinking of investing in, and only selected the ones with the highest Test rating. After a few years, he was able to move his family into one of the best houses in town, and give them all the luxuries he had never been able to get them before.

## WHAT ULTRA-PICTRONICS CAN DO FOR YOU

Ultra-Pictronics, as you have just seen, releases your full materialization power . . . power that has been chained up inside you since babyhood. Now, for the first time, you're going to be able to "will" things into existence . . . to have all the money you want . . . whenever you feel like it. After a bit of practice, Ultra-Pictronics will be as natural to you as breathing . . . and just as easy.

In this chapter, you've discovered:

- The secret of Ultra-Glyphics that helps you concentrate your desires on one object until it comes to you freely.

- The secret of Verbal Invocation that brings you the things you want . . . just for the asking.

- The secret of Graphic Invocation that turns an ordinary letter into a charged instrument with awesome powers.

- The secret of Psychonic Repetology and the Command Ray that make others do the things you want.

- The secret of Ultronic Multiplication that literally changes your luck from bad to good . . . and makes you a winner in any game of chance.

- The secret of the Luctronic Test that works like a compass to guide you unerringly to the big money.

- The secret of the Lottery Nest that pours winning vibrations into any lottery, sweepstake or raffle ticket you may hold.

- The secret of the Astral Spur that changes the odds in your favor, and makes dice and horseraces work in your favor.

- And the most useful Secret of all . . . the mighty Secret of Reverse Money-Flow that brings back every dollar you spend, so that your money is never used up!

These are but a few of the many applications of Ultra-Pictronics toward building your personal fortune. You can use one, two or all of them to get the things you want. The more of them you use, the faster things will happen for you.

Naturally, if you use them in conjunction with other techniques in this book, they'll work that much better. Using Ultra-Hypnology along with the Command Ray when you go in to ask for a raise, for example, will make getting the raise that much faster and easier.

And, finally, other techniques you'll read about in the pages to come will show you how to use the riches you've gained for a fuller, happier and more rewarding life.

# 4

## ULTRA-MNEMONICS:
### How to
### Have a Perfect
### Memory

---

How good is your memory? Most people are convinced that their memories are weak . . . they can hardly remember what they had for dinner last night, much less anything important.

Yet Ultra-Mnemonics says otherwise, and so do many leading mind-scientists. Some go so far as to claim that the human mind never forgets *anything* . . . that deep in the recesses of your brain is everything that has ever happened to you, waiting only for the right key to unlock it.

### Activating Your Ultra-Psychonic Memory Circuits

One of the most fascinating things memory experts have found out about so-called "loss of memory" is, in many cases, it has not really taken place.

A student for example, is faced with a tough problem on a test. "I just can't remember how to do it," he thinks. But, in reality, the information was never in his mind in the first place. Perhaps he skipped that page in his text, or wasn't paying attention when it was brought up in class. Either way, the basic principle remains the same: *you cannot remember something you did not know before.*

This sounds simple—yet millions of people convince themselves every day that they have poor memories because they cannot remember information they never had to begin with.

So the first step in activating your Ultra-Psychonic memory circuits is to run a memory-check. If you can't remember a particular item, you must ask yourself if you really knew it earlier. You'll find that it is embarrassingly easy to check this out—just concentrate on when, where and how you were given the information that you're trying to recall. If you can't remember acquiring the information, it means that you never did.

The most significant thing about this fact is its converse: if you can remember learning something, it is available to you fully and completely. Recently, scientists conducted tests with aged hospital patients. Some of them could not even remember their names, and did not know where they were. By giving them doses of a chemical called DNA, their mental channels were completely cleared in a few days, and they returned to normal. Some of them, in fact, were able to remember such long-forgotten things as the names of their classmates from half a century before!

Luckily, most people do not need a dose of DNA to improve their memories. You can get just as good, or better results, by using the techniques of Ultra-Mnemonics to train and sharpen your memory powers.

In the next few pages, you are going to discover:

- The astounding Memory Mirror that lets you look far back into the past, and recall facts you've forgotten for years!

- The powerful Instant Replay technique that strengthens your "memory muscles" and turns you into a Memory Giant!

- The amazing Ultronic Memory-House that stores thousands of facts and figures for you in the simplest way imaginable!

- The startling technique of Graphic Mnemonics that makes a pencil and paper equal to the mightiest computer!

- The fantastic Psychonic Memory Sphere that makes you a mental wizard, and releases your Fourth-Dimensional memory booster!

- The secret of Reincarnal Recall that lets you draw on memories from previous lives!
- The miracle of Ultra-Akashic Memory that makes objects "speak" to you and tell you what they have seen.

If you are willing to spend as little as five minutes a day practicing these techniques, they can all be yours.

## The Astounding Memory Mirror

How many times have you looked in an ordinary mirror and seen your face reflected there? Suppose there was a similar mirror in your mind . . . a mirror that would reflect the past in full detail, making it possible to recall even the most obscure, long-forgotten items . . . what would you give for such a mirror?

Well, there really *is* such a mirror in your mind, and the techniques of Ultra-Mnemonics make it available to you just for the asking.

Here's how it works:

Suppose you want to remember the name of a man you met a year ago, and you can't seem to think of it.

Instead of just giving up, like most people do, try this step-by-step Memory Mirror technique:

1. Write down on a sheet of paper all the things you think of when you try to remember the name—

> Morton
> Mimu
> Noomi
> Newton

2. Now lie down quietly for five minutes and generate an egonic flow, as explained in Chapter 1.

3. Imagine this egonic flow is turning on a tiny computer inside your mind. See the dials start to move, the tapes start to spin, the lights blinking off and on.

4. With a mental "finger," press the button marked Memory Mirror on the computer keyboard.

5. Now look at your list again. Start adding names once more:

> Noonan
> Morman
> Newly
> Human

Newman
NEWMAN!

That's it! Suddenly, it all comes back to you. Mr. Newman appears in your memory, standing there, shaking your hand, and telling you his name.

The main thing to remember in using this technique is that you must permit yourself "free association"—that is, let your mind roam freely, and write down whatever words come into it, no matter how strange or unusual they sound.

## How Vincent U. Remembered a Vital Piece
## of Information and Won His Case

A recent court case I came across demonstrates the value of the Memory Mirror technique.

Vincent U., a restaurant worker, was driving home late one night after work when suddenly a car ran through a stop light and smashed into him.

The only witness was an elderly man in a car behind Vincent's. He told Vincent he would be happy to testify in his favor when the case came to court. Vincent was so shook up from the crash, however, that he failed to write down the man's name and address.

The case *did* go to court, and the other driver claimed it was all Vincent's fault. It looked bad for Vincent, because the other driver was a wealthy local politician, and his word seemed to count more with the jury than that of a poor restaurant worker.

Luckily, Vincent's lawyer knew about the Memory Mirror technique, and persuaded Vincent to try it. To Vincent's great surprise, in just half an hour the whole accident came back to him in complete detail, and the name and address of the witness popped into his mind.

Confronted with the witness, the other driver's lawyer immediately asked the court for a recess, and when it was over, told the judge that his client had settled the case out of court. Vincent U. got back every penny he had lost, as well as several thousand dollars for pain and suffering.

## The Secret of Ultra-Psychic Memory Improvement

If you're like most of us, you're probably not happy with

your memory. Perhaps you meet people who greet you by name, yet who seem to be perfect strangers. Perhaps you get annoyed when you can't remember where you put something, or because you frequently seem to "lose" things you need. Perhaps you get aggravated when you have to spend long minutes looking up facts and figures you know you should have at your fingertips. Or perhaps you get that frustrated feeling when a good idea or a clever remark seems to slip away from you, and you just can't seem to get it back.

Good as it is, the Memory Mirror technique takes time—sometimes only a few minutes, it's true—but there are occasions when you just can't wait—when you need "instant answers." How can you strengthen and improve your memory to achieve this?

There are two basically different approaches to Ultra-Psychonic Memory Improvement—one, purely mental; and the other, using physical aids.

Unlike old-fashioned "rote" memory, where you were simply told to repeat something over and over again until you could repeat it perfectly, Ultra-Psychonic Memory Improvement is based on the discoveries made by psychologists on how the human mind works. It turns the whole process into a pleasant game instead of a boring chore, and uses multi-sensory inputs to speed the data-storing process.

What's more, the recall process is reinforced by the use of the "reward principle"—a magic device that makes remembering as enjoyable as possible.

Here are the techniques that will do this for you:

## The Instant Replay Technique

Have you ever seen an instant replay on TV? A few seconds after an event, the whole thing is repeated exactly as it happened.

A simple procedure—but one that can strengthen your memory enormously when you apply the idea via Ultra-Psychonics.

This is how you make it work for you:

1. Select an area you pass by frequently during the course of your average day. It could be a street with several stores on it, it could be a kitchen cabinet or a bookcase. What matters is that the area should contain a large collection of different objects.

2. The next time you pass this area, select one section of it. You might choose a store window, for example.

3. Stare steadily at the store window for exactly 30 seconds, trying to remember as much as possible about what you see inside it.

4. Turn on your Egonic Computer, as you did for the Memory Mirror, and imagine you are recording the entire scene on tape, just like a TV camera.

5. Now turn away from the area you've memorized, and try to see how much of it you can recall. Suppose you had been looking into a hardware store window, for example. How many hammers were there? How many saws? How many electric drills? What color were they? What prices were they marked? Where were they placed in relation to each other? And so on—until you have recalled every fact you possibly can.

6. Next, look back at the area and see how many things you got right. You'll be delighted by how much you've managed to recall. (This is the "reward" principle I mentioned earlier.)

7. The following day, repeat the exact same ritual. This time, you'll find you've managed to remember even more items in the window.

8. Do this for at least two weeks, until every item in the store window (or whatever other area you've selected) is crystal clear in your mind.

9. Now select another area, and repeat the entire Instant Replay game again.

10. After doing this seven or eight times, you'll feel a definite strengthening of your memory. It will get easier and easier for you to look at even the most confused collection of objects and quickly lock them into your memory banks.

And that's all there is to it—a simple, easy and pleasant way to train your memory that builds it up and makes it stronger, just as lifting weights day after day will build up your muscles.

## How Seymour C. Got a Promotion

The effectiveness of the Instant Replay technique can be

more fully appreciated when you see how it has helped others.

Take Seymour C., for example. For several years he had been an order filler in a large camera store. His job was to find, among the thousands of items on shelves in the store basement, the particular item that a salesman would call down for.

All day long, the intercom system would call him: "Hey, Seymour, send up a package of Kodak 120 color film!" . . . "Seymour, I need a 12-inch Bradley trimmer. Send it up right away!" And so on, with literally thousands of different photo items involved—some as small as a pea.

Seymour had tried for several years to cope with this job, but he couldn't seem to get anywhere. Writing things down didn't help much, because things were constantly being moved around. As a result, he was making a salary just above the minimum wage, and worried constantly about getting fired for being so slow in doing his job.

Then he discovered the Instant Replay technique. Within a few weeks, he was able to find any item the salesmen requested in seconds. Two months later, he became head of the Order Department, and shortly thereafter moved up to a high-paying salesman's job. In less than a year, he had tripled his salary!

### The Ultronic Memory House

"Well," you may say, "the Instant Replay technique is certainly a great method for training your memory to collect the data, but what's the best way to store all those facts?"

And that is a very good point. Unless you have a memory that can be tapped quickly and easily, the ability to put things into it is of only limited use.

That is why Ultra-Mnemonics has developed the "Memory House" storage system. It keeps each one of your memories separate and distinct, and lets you refer to them instantly, as easily as walking from one room to another.

And that's exactly how it works. In your mind, you construct an imaginary house with 10 big empty rooms in it. Then, you move in the "furniture"—your present stock of memories, which you divide up to fit the various categories each room contains.

New memories are stored in the same set of "rooms." And recall becomes amazingly simple. Just as you know that food is usually kept in the kitchen, for example, you know that recipes would also be kept there. Thus, to remember a particular recipe, you mentally stroll into the kitchen of your Memory House and find the recipe you want in just seconds.

Here's what the Ultronic Memory House looks like:

*1. LIVING ROOM:* Reception Center for New Data—Storage Planning—Memory Retrieval Area

*2. PARLOR:* E.S.P. Center—Magic Spells—Telepathy—Religion—Advanced Psychonic Powers

*3. BATHROOM:* Health—Longevity —Beauty—Rejuvenation—Herbs— Unpleasant Memory Deletion

*4. KITCHEN:* Food—Taste—Smell— Recipes — Entertainment Plans — Drinks—Diets—Laundry

*5. DINING ROOM:* Family—Relatives—Friends—People—Birthdays —Phone Numbers—Addresses

6. GARAGE: Automobiles — Home Repair—Mechanical Things—Painting—Gardening—Pets

*7. STUDY:* School—Childhood Memories — Math — Science — Art — Languages—Social Studies

*8. DEN:* Hobbies — Sports — Books — Records — Collections — Games — Writing—Family History—Music

*9. OFFICE:* Bills—Taxes—Jobs—Purchases — Money-Making Plans — Investments—Calculations

*10. BEDROOM:* Dreams—Love—Sex— Clothing — Travel — Vacations — Parties—Kids—Security

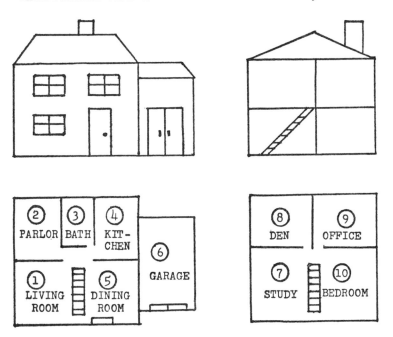

## How to Store Key Data in Your Permanent Memory Bank

It's all yours—and you can make each room as big or as small as you like. Here's how you use it:

Imagine you are sitting in your living room. People deliver things at the front door, and you get up and put them away. You watch TV or read a newspaper—perhaps you write down an important fact or clip something of interest out of the news-paper—and then put it in one of the rooms.

And that's all there is to it. As new data comes into your mind, you simply sort it out, decide where you're going to keep it and put it away in one of your mental "rooms."

To remember the item, you simply think of where it would be—just as you would look for your socks in the bedroom—and mentally walk into that "room" and retrieve it.

The process has already started. As you read these words, your mind is starting to transfer your entire stock of memories into your brand-new Ultronic Memory House. Pause for a moment, and enjoy the sensation of everything in your mind being sorted out and put away neatly in the various "rooms."

"But," you say, "I have some memories that don't fit any of the categories you've listed." That's the great advantage of the Ultronic Memory House—the "rooms" can be as big or small as you like. You simply select the room that seems to come closest to your "extra" memories—and just put them there.

For instance, a single man who has spent most of his life as a sailor would have an entirely different set of mental "furniture" than a young married woman who teaches school in Illinois.

But the Ultronic Memory House is big enough for both. No matter what kind of mental "furniture" you stock it with, you'll find it enormously easier to remember things, and to recall them in a flash—automatically.

Think of it this way: most people keep all their memories piled up in a giant heap. Imagine such a heap of furniture and household items piled up on a vacant lot. Imagine chairs piled on top of beds, blankets and cans of food all mixed together with important papers and empty beer cans. That's what an unsorted memory is like.

Now, contrast that with a neatly arranged house where everything is in its proper place. If you want to find something, you just walk right into the room where it is and pick it up.

If you needed something in a hurry, which would be easier to look through—the house or the junkpile?

And that is the basic reason the Ultronic Memory House must work for you. It may not be "perfect"—but it's a vast improvement over the way things are now.

## How Lila B. Became a Social Leader in Her Community

Ever since Lila B. had moved into her neighborhood, people had become increasingly unfriendly to her. She got fewer and fewer invitations, less and less phone calls—even her Christmas cards started to drop off. Finally, in desperation, she asked Mary, one of her few remaining friends, to tell her what she was doing wrong.

"Lila," said Mary, "you're a nice person. But you never seem to remember the little things about people that make them friendly."

"Like what," said Lila.

"Like their names, their kids, their husbands, their hobbies, to name just a few. Only last week you insulted Mrs. D to her face, right in front of two of her best friends, by asking how her husband was."

"What was so terrible about that?"

"She's been suing him for divorce for over a month now."

"Oh! I forgot," said Lila.

"Sure you did," Mary told her, "and guess who *she's* going to forget when she makes up her next party list."

"What can I do?" cried Lila.

"If I were you, I'd get my memory fixed," said Mary.

Shortly after this, Lila heard about the Ultronic Memory House technique and decided to give it a try. To her surprise, the very next day she made a hit with it. She said hello to one of the town's leading women, and remembered to ask about her son in college. Before she knew it, the woman was talking a blue streak to her, and even invited her to come over for coffee that evening.

One by one, Lila B. regained all her lost friends and gained many new ones. Before she knew it, she was one of the most popular and respected people in town.

## Graphic Mnemonics: The Incredible New Way to Recall Names, Faces, Facts and Figures in a Flash

If you can count to five, you can use an amazingly simple, yet enormously effective way to remember names, faces, facts and figures called Graphic Mnemonics.

You've seen how the Ultronic Memory House arranges your memories in simple, logical order that makes finding any particular item a snap. Now, with Graphic Mnemonics, you can put these instantly available memories to work for you in a wide variety of situations.

Graphic Mnemonics lets you assemble these memories into short, useful groups. Here's how it works:

1. Select the five most important facts about any given item and write them down on a sheet of paper. Suppose you're a teacher—pick one of your pupils and write down:

A. John Harrington
B. Well-behaved
C. IQ 97
D. Hard-working
E. Eight absences

2. Now, put the whole item *as a unit* into one of the "rooms" of your Ultronic Memory House. In this case, it would go into the Office, Room 9.

3. Repeat the procedure for another student.

4. Continue doing this until you have reached five students.

5. Now, in your mind, combine all five into one unit.

6. Continue doing this, combining things into units of five.

7. Now, combine the units of five into larger collections of five units each.

8. Continue this process until all the items are taken care of. That's all there is to it.

To bring back the information, hold your right hand in front of you. Each finger stands first, for all the items in the largest collection units you've used. Select the appropriate finger.

Find the unit the item is in. Since it's all neatly arranged in your mind, this should take only a few seconds.

Then find the subunit the same way. Continue until you have reached the level you're looking for. In the illustration we used, the teacher would look at her hand again during the last step, and all the information about the particular student would immediately come into her mind.

Think of how handy this would be if you had to remember key facts about 200 or 300 students! Or if you had to remember a lot of formulas; or recipes; or anything else where you have a large collection of items with a similar set of characteristics.

## How Peter E. Became Sales Manager

Peter E. can testify to the effectiveness of this method. He was just a struggling, low-paid salesman till he tried it. Within a few weeks, he was able to improve his performance dramatically. Not only did he know his line backwards and forwards, and the advantages and disadvantages of his competitors' lines, but he was able to remember the key facts about each of the hundreds of people he dealt with—a talent that made him welcome as a friend wherever he went. His salary and commissions rose rapidly from $5,000 a year to $10,000 and then to $20,000. Finally, he was promoted to sales manager at $35,000 a year. And he's still going up, he reports.

## Amazing Psychonic Memory Sphere Makes You a Mental Wizard

Now you've just seen how it is possible to "compress" your memories—actually make one memory do the work of five. Suppose there was a way to also increase your memory storage by 50% or 100%—think of how it would multiply your brainpower. You'd be, in effect, a true Mental Wizard.

Well, there is such a way. It's called the Psychonic Memory Sphere, and it takes only a few minutes to master it. Basically, it's just a way of changing your mental outlook.

You see, most people store their memories in two dimensions. Think of the Ultronic Memory House. Have you been storing your memories in a two-dimensional, flat diagram?

Now, try this. Imagine each room has three full dimensions, just like a real room does. Suddenly, you find you have 50% more room than you did before—you see ways to hang memory units on the "walls," store them over and under each other and stack them neatly in related piles.

The next step is a bit more subtle. Study the diagram below for a moment:

What you're looking at is a picture of the various ways your mind can store its memories. The top half of the picture shows how much memory storage you have in each dimension. Thus, if you could store two facts in one dimension (1-D), you could store four facts in two dimensions (2-D). If you expand your thinking into three dimensions (3D), as you did at the start of this section, you double the storage capacity again, to eight facts.

Obviously, if you could expand your mind into four dimensions (4-D), you could double the capacity once more, to 16 facts!

"But," you say, "how can I do this? I'm only a 3-D being."

The answer is simple—you've just done it! Just as looking at a 2-D drawing of a 3-D object extends your mind, via your imagination, into an extra dimension, so, too, looking at a drawing of a 4-D object extends your mind the same way.

The bottom half of the diagram shows a single memory cell in each of the various dimensions we've just talked about. As you look at the last drawing—the 4-D sphere (or hypersphere, as it is sometimes called)—every memory cell in your mind is extending itself—via your imagination—into the fourth dimension. You have just doubled your memory capacity!

All that remains for you to do is take full advantage of the 4-D Psychonic Memory Sphere—the total storage capacity of all your 4-D memory cells. Start transferring memories into it now, using the techniques you've already learned.

### How Stanley L. Won His Election

The usefulness of this technique became quite apparent to a local politician, Stanley L. Not only was he able to remember the faces, names and key facts about scores of key political leaders and potential contributors, but in debate with his opponents, he was able to recall every political mistake they'd ever made, and flatten them. He was recently re-elected by an overwhelming majority.

### The Secret of Language Mastery

How would you like to be able to speak and write a dozen different languages? If I can do it, so can you. And with the help of Ultra-Psychonics, it becomes child's play.

The 4-D Psychonic Memory Sphere readily lends itself to this sort of thing. You can easily master and store thousands of new words and expressions in your Ultronic Memory House, in as many languages as you like. What's more, you can keep each one separate and distinct, and you can draw on them quickly and automatically whenever you wish.

"But," you say, "I'm busy. I can't devote much time to it."

The answer will delight you. You can learn these languages in as little as seven minutes a day. Here's how you do it:

1. Get yourself a good grammar book of the language you want to learn. You can find them in any bookstore, or save money by looking around in second-hand bookshops. Or you can even take them out of your local public library, if you can figure out a way to keep renewing them.

2. Every day allow yourself exactly seven minutes for learning the language. During this time, you concentrate on learning exactly seven words—no more, no less. Early in the morning is the best time.

3. Between that time and the next day, you think about the words during your spare moments—perhaps while waiting for a bus or doing the dishes.

4. Just before you go to sleep every night, have one last review. Then, consciously transfer the words into one of the rooms in your Ultronic Memory House, and place them in your 4-D Psychonic Memory Sphere.

Which room? It depends on how you have your Memory House organized. However, it takes only one simple act of visualization to put a 4-D Psychonic Memory Sphere in *every* room, so there's no problem.

Practice this technique every day for a year, and you will have mastered any language you want. Take Chinese, for example. If you learn just seven words a day for a year, you will know 3,255 words of Chinese. According to experts, if you know just 1,500 Chinese words, you can read 95% of a Chinese daily newspaper. Of course, Chinese is a difficult language, since you must memorize a symbol to go along with each word. Most languages are much easier—even a few months of effort can make you fairly fluent in them.

## How Philip and Gloria F. Saved
## Thousands of Dollars on Their Trip

Does learning another language pay off? A couple I know

thinks so. They took a trip to Italy a few years ago, and because they had taken the trouble to learn Italian this simple way, their trip turned into a "dream" vacation. It wasn't just that they saved money—although they were able to cut the cost of their vacation almost in half. They also found that they could order delicacies that the ordinary tourist didn't even know about, that they could read museum labels and street signs, that they could order train and theater tickets, and above all, talk to the warm-hearted, generous Italians who gave them a special welcome because they could speak their language. And did they save money! They stayed at a splendid deluxe hotel for $10 a night, while the average tourist was paying double that or else staying in a fleabag. They got into museums for half-price with a special card that was almost impossible to get if you couldn't speak the language. They ate like royalty in little restaurants that the tourist books never mention— but which cost half of what the big-name tourist traps charge. They were able to shop the sales in Italian stores and save money on everything from fine gloves to Florentine jewelry. They told me that, in effect, a $5,000 trip had cost them a little under $2,400.

## BEYOND THE GATES OF MEMORY

There are other types of memory beyond the conventional kind, and until now, they have never been able to be linked to ordinary memory processes. Here is how they tie-in with Ultra-Psychonics:

### How to Tap Reincarnal Recall
### and Talk to the Racial Mind

Reincarnal Recall means—quite simply—tapping the memories of your ancestors. There are many cases on record of this, including the famous Bridey Murphy incident of some years ago. What actually happens is this: the subject accidentally energizes his 4-D Psychonic Memory Sphere. The Fourth Dimension has sometimes been described as the Time Dimension, and perhaps this may enable the subject's mind to move along the time-track into the distant past. If this is so, it should also be possible to move ahead far into the future and tap the ultimate Racial Mind of Humanity.

Try this experiment: Tonight, before you go to sleep, select a particular ancestor you want to contact. Then, as you slip off into sleep, imagine that your Psychonic Memory Sphere is moving backward in Time. When you awaken in the morning, make a quick note on a piece of paper as to what you can remember about your dreams.

Similarly, to contact the Racial Mind, imagine that your Psychonic Memory Sphere is moving forward in Time. Try to visualize the final human race—all linked telepathically into one giant Brain. Think of a question to ask it. Again, record your answer next morning.

There's no guarantee that this will work right away. In fact, for some people it just won't work at all. But for most people, one or two tries should give you a unique psychic experience.

## Secrets of Akashic Memory and the Voices of the Past

Some people have unusual mystical powers. They can hold an ordinary object—a stone, a piece of wood, a metal artifact— in their hand—and actually "feel" its memories—hear the Voices of the Past speak out and tell them the history of the object.

Everyone has this power to some extent—think of how you shudder a little when you see a famous gun or the scene of a famous battle. But here's a technique that may help you to improve your akashic powers:

Pick up an object that you know the history of—an old shoe, for example—and hold it in your hand while you sit in an easy chair completely relaxed. Let your Psychonic Memory Sphere start to feed memories about the object into your mind. Remember when you first saw the object, what it looked like when it was new, what you did with it when you brought it home and so on. Now try to "remember" what happened to it before you ever saw it. Try to visualize it being made, being shipped to where you got it and similar things. To your surprise, you may feel strange new memories slipping in—memories you didn't expect. They'll be very faint, at first, and it will take a great deal of effort just to become aware of them.

These are the first stirrings of your Akashic Memory. Keep practicing this skill regularly, and it will become stronger and stronger. Try other objects, going always from the known to the unknown. You'll be surprised at how fast this talent develops!

## WHAT ULTRA-MNEMONICS CAN DO FOR YOU

In this chapter, you have discovered:

- How to activate your Ultra-Psychonic Memory Circuits with the astounding Memory Mirror Technique.
- How to use the Instant Replay Technique to strengthen your "memory muscles."
- How to store your present set of memories in a well-organized, easily accessible Ultronic Memory House.
- How to recall names, faces, facts and figures in the twinkling of an eye with Graphic Mnemonics.
- How to expand your memory storage capacity 100% by use of the amazing Psychonic Memory Sphere.
- How to master any language you want to learn in just seven minutes a day.
- How to reach back in time with Reincarnal Recall and communicate with your long-departed ancestors.
- How to move forward in time and get help from the ultimate Racial Mind of Man.
- How to listen to the Voices of the Past that speak out from inanimate objects and discover their history.

Make a particular effort to master the techniques in this chapter, and you'll discover that not only will the rest of this book become easier to understand and use, but your daily life will take a dramatic turn for the better!

# 5

## ULTRA-GENIOLOGY:
## How to
## Multiply Your Brainpower
## 1,000 Times

---

The mightiest power on Earth is about to be placed into your hands—the power of Thought. This is the Force that raised man from the beasts and gave him dominion over all living things—the surging energy that can level mountains and travel to the farthest star in the twinkling of an eye.

Prepare to receive the secrets that will transform you into a superior being with vastly expanded brainpower and an entirely new outlook on the Universe.

### The Secret of Geniologic

What is it that makes one person different from another? Why is it that John A. is considered a brilliant, clever, advanced thinker while John B. is considered to be a clod?

Both have the same brains, yet one person is able to use them much more effectively than the other. It's as if a piano were in both their houses—John A. has taken the trouble to learn to play it, while John B. has just been ignoring it.

Yet, it's perfectly obvious to an outsider that all John B. has to do is sit down at the piano, take some lessons and he can become an accomplished player. Provided, of course, that he puts a little effort into it.

The same is true of your brain. If you are willing to take a few simple lessons in how to use the marvelous instrument that you possess, you will be astonished at what it can do.

For example:

- You'll see how to have more time to do the things you want—and still have plenty of time left over!

- You'll see how your own 10 fingers can be made to do the work of an electronic computer—only faster and better!

- You'll discover how you can solve any problem that faces you in half the time it would normally take!

- You'll see how you can absorb information five times faster than you do now—and get more out of it!

- You'll discover a new way to create ideas that can make you rich—a technique that can bring you enormous sums of money virtually overnight!

- You'll see how a paper and pencil can multiply your brainpower by a factor of 1,000—or more!

- You'll discover a new way of using your mind that actually lets you think of two things at once!

- You'll find out about a mysterious "network" that can work miracles for you!

- You'll discover the amazing secret of the Mental Organon—a mighty mental engine that will roar into action at your command!

- You'll see the six-fold path that leads to total mental control, and gives you, in effect, a "super-brain"!

- And you'll find out how even this tremendous new brainpower can be multiplied further!

This, in short, is the secret of Geniologic, or Ultra-Genio-ology. Step-by-step, the ultronic, psychonic and egonic powers of your mind are going to be trained to do your bidding, and produce results that right now you may think are impossible. Yet, these results—these fantastic powers—are yours for the asking.

## How to Tap the Mysterious Power
## of Interstitial Time

How many times have you come home and found a potentially great evening ruined by a stack of chores that have piled up, and can't be put off any more? Or wished you had more time to read a book or go for a walk?

Perhaps you've been wasting a substance I call "interstitial time." It consists of little bits and pieces of time that most people "lose"—time that they can never have again—and yet which is thrown away, second by second, until hours, days and weeks are gone forever.

For example, suppose you have to leave for work at 8 a.m. and you find you're ready at 7:55 a.m. Most people completely waste the extra five minutes—they talk to someone, look out the window or just sit around. Yet, suppose they decided to use this time to pay a bill—or perhaps address an envelope—or throw out some old magazines.

That evening, when they return, they've picked up five *extra* minutes—minutes they can spend doing anything they want. Suppose they decide to "reinvest" this time, and add to it all the wasted minutes they now spend watching TV commercials. Perhaps they might find time to clean part of the house, or wash the dishes, or fix something that's broken.

Imagine you've done this all week. When the weekend rolls around, you suddenly find yourself free to do more of the things you want. You have more time to go out, to shop, to visit friends, or to do anything else you desire.

Yet there are still the same number of hours in a day—only your "minute-stretcher" has made the difference.

These are the basic rules for using your "interstitial time" most effectively:

1. Decide right now that you are not going to waste even one second of your time.

2. Work out a plan on how to use it. For example, if you have 10 minutes free every morning before you go to work, and you want to use it to learn French, plan on where you will keep your books and papers so that you can get at them in just a few seconds.

3. Make up a list of projects you want to do. For instance, if you've been planning to put those photos of last year's vacation in your scrapbook, put it on the list.

4. Figure out how you can work on the projects in little bits and pieces of time, instead of all at once. This is easier than it seems. Suppose you want to paint a room. You can move things out of the room a little at a time for days in advance. You can put down papers or a dropcloth in a few minutes. You can prepare a plastic coverall to slip into for short 10-minute painting sessions. And you can put things back a little bit at a time, the same way.

There are very few things you can't do this way. But you'll find you have more than enough time to do them, too—because you'll be saving hours and even days on everything else.

### Ultronic Counting: How to Have 1,000 Fingers

Anyone can count on their fingers to 10—but how would you like to be able to count from 1 to 1,000 on the same 10 fingers?

Suppose there were only two numbers: 1 and 0. Instead of being able to count 1, 2, 3, 4, 5, 6, 7, 8, 9, 10, 11, 12, etc., you'd have to count much more simply: 1, 10, 11, 100, 101, 110, 111, 1,000, etc.

Here is how these numbers would translate into regular numbers:

$$1=1$$
$$2=10$$
$$3=11$$
$$4=100$$
$$5=101$$
$$6=110$$
$$7=111$$
$$8=1000$$
$$9=1001$$

and so on. The principle here is that $1 + 0 = 1$ and $1 + 1 = 10$. You can extend the list as far as you'd like.

How do you apply it to your fingers? Simple: an extended finger stands for 1, a closed finger stands for 0.

Here's how you would count in Ultronic Finger Counting:

$$1=00000\ 00001$$
$$2=00000\ 00010$$
$$3=00000\ 00011$$
$$4=00000\ 00100$$
$$5=00000\ 00101$$
$$6=00000\ 00110$$
$$7=00000\ 00111$$
$$8=00000\ 01000$$
$$9=00000\ 01001$$

In other words, if the index finger of your right hand were extended, you would be indicating the number 8. The index finger and pinky of your right hand extended would be 9. And, if all the fingers on both hands were extended, the number 11111 11111 stands for 1,023. As you can see by using this method, it is possible to count to over 1,000, using nothing more than your 10 fingers!

Of course, it takes a little practice to do this easily, to get some of your fingers used to bending this way. But once you've done it, you've added a tremendous new talent to your life.

You can, for example, add faster than an electronic computer. Suppose you want to add 4 plus 8, for example. You know that 4 is 00000 00100 and that 8 is 00000 01000. You simply combine them on your fingers in one operation, and get 00000 01100, which is 12. This is a lot faster than punching out the numbers on a calculating machine, and then punching a totalling key for the answer.

The reason that this method works so well is that your brain works the same way. Everything is stored in it as an electric charge—in other words, it is all either 1 (charged) or 0 (not charged). When you calculate this way on your fingers, you set up a direct link between them and your brain!

## How Frank D. Won a $100 Bet

A friend of mine, Frank D., won $100 this way from a stranger who bet him that he couldn't keep track of the number of people coming into a hotel lobby they were sitting in, in Florida. The other man kept up a running stream of conversation to distract him, but Frank simply held the tally on his fingers, using the Ultronic Counting secret you've just learned, and then added in new arrivals as they entered. After an hour, the stranger checked out Frank's tally with an actual on-the-spot count. To his surprise, Frank was 100% right—and the stranger lost the bet.


### Invoking the Psychonic Image

Another technique for multiplying your brainpower is to invoke the Psychonic Image. What this means, in practical terms, is that you construct a "model" of any problem you face, and then solve it on a smaller scale.

For example, suppose you are giving a dinner party, and it's important to seat your guests in a certain way. Let's say that you want to:

(1) alternate men and women around the table

(2) put Mrs. Jones as far away as possible from her ex-hus-
band

(3) put several young single people next to each other

(4) put your oldest friends near you at the head of the table

(5) put people with similar occupations and hobbies together

(6) allow for certain people possibly not showing up

Now this would be very hard to do, if all you have to work with is a guest list. But if you make a small paper Psychonic Image model of the table, and write up small cards with the key data for each guest, you can solve the problem easily by switching the cards around the model until the problem is solved.

Another example of using this technique might be in planning your vacation. By making up Psychonic Image models of the key places you want to cover, you can set things up so that you'll be able to see more, do more and get the most out of your limited time.

Suppose you decide to visit New York City on your vacation, and you want to see many more things than you know you have time for. You might want to see 30 or 40 places, for instance, and figure you have time enough to see only 20 of them.

To use the Psychonic Image technique, you would make up 30 or 40 cards like this:

| OPEN | CLOSED | HOURS | COST | LOCATION |
|------|--------|-------|------|----------|
| WEATHER | PLACE: | | | TRAVEL |
| RATING<br>*** Must<br>** Want<br>* Like | FEATURES | SPECIAL | NEAR | TRAVEL $ |

Here's a filled-out Psychonic Image card:

| OPEN | CLOSED | HOURS | COST | LOCATION |
|------|--------|-------|------|----------|
| EVERY DAY | LEGAL HOLIDAYS | 10-5 MON-SAT 1-5 SUN | $1.00 | ON 5TH AVENUE AT EAST 82ND ST |
| WEATHER<br>OK FOR RAINY DAY | PLACE:<br>METROPOLITAN MUSEUM OF ART<br>5TH AVE + 82ND ST.<br>TR9-5500 | | | TRAVEL<br>5TH AVE BUS TO E. 82 ST. |
| RATING<br>⬤*** Must<br>** Want<br>* Like | FEATURES<br>PAINTINGS SCULPTURE | SPECIAL<br>VAN GOGH SHOW 7/3-7/17 | NEAR<br>CENTRAL PARK ZOO | TRAVEL $<br>70¢<br>ROUND TRIP |

As you can see, it lets you account for every possible factor, including how badly you want to see any particular sight. Once you've filled out cards for all the places you want to see, it's a simple matter to arrange them and line up the places you want to see most, so that you'll be sure to get to them. In fact, if you line them up carefully enough, you may even be able to squeeze in four or five "extra" sights you thought you wouldn't have time for.

Another advantage is that you can take the cards on your trip and make last-minute changes to allow for strikes, bad weather, etc.

### How Esther W. Became Office Manager

Esther W., a low-paid secretary, put this technique to good effect when her boss asked her to help him rearrange the people in the outer office. Not only did she make Psychonic Image models of the desks and furniture, but she marked her people-cards with facts about personality, work enthusiasm, punctuality and other key data that enabled her to make an arrangement that actually increased the office's output by 20%. Her boss was so impressed with her work that shortly thereafter she was promoted to Office Manager, and doubled her salary!

### Ultra-Readology: How to Read Five Times Faster in Five Minutes

Another way to multiply your brainpower is to speed up your reading rate. Most people read at about one-fifth the speed they can attain with a little training in Ultra-Readology.

Try these five Ultra-Readology techniques, and see how your mental powers are increased:

1. As you continue to read this book, put one finger on either side of your Adam's apple. If you feel a vibration as you read, it means you are *subvocalizing* the words. This slows you down enormously when you read, but it can be easily eliminated. Keeping your fingers on your throat, blow air out through your lips as you read. Practice this for five minutes a day, and you'll find that this subvocalization habit can be quickly broken for good.

2. The next step is to develop your powers of Peripheral Vision. If you stare at something directly in front of you, you not only see it, but objects to the right and left of it. This ability to see out of the corners of your eyes is called Peripheral Vision, and once you become aware of it, you can speed your reading considerably. What it means to you is this: instead of scanning each line you read from beginning to end, stop about 1/2-inch short on either side. (To make sure you do not move your head, hold your chin between your thumb and forefinger, until you

break the habit.) Now, each time you read a line, your eyes travel 1 inch less. This does not seem like much, until you realize that there are 40 lines or so to the average page. In other words, this one technique saves your eyes from covering a distance of over *3½ feet* on each page! Multiply that by the length of a book, and you can see how much time this saves you. Practice this for five minutes every day, and watch your reading speed pick up.

3. Next, we come to the Ultronic Scanning Accelerator. Strange as it may sound, researchers have found that people's eyes do not travel across a line in one continuous sweep, but in groups of words. Most people stop slightly at least three or four times a line. Concentrate on changing this. Try to move your eyes across a line in just two jumps. Remember, there is *no limit* to the size of the group of words your eyes can send to your mind. Practice this for five minutes a day, and you will double your reading speed.

4. For the next step, you set up a "psychonic cyclotron" inside your mind, as previously explained in Chapter 1. Keep it spinning at a constant speed as you read this line. Now, as you move on to the next line, imagine that it is spinning *twice* as fast—and that you are reading twice as fast, too. Don't worry if you do not pick up every single word—most languages consist of 50% or more "noise" words. For instance, take the sentence "I am a farmer." Cut out the two middle words, and you have "I—farmer." It's not elegant, but the meaning is still there, and that's all you need. In fact, tests have shown that when you read faster, you usually understand better, even if you miss a word or two. Again, practice five minutes each day until the faster reading speed becomes automatic.

5. The other great stumbling block to faster reading is a poor vocabulary. No matter how fast you read, if you do not know the meaning of enough of the words, the material you've read will not make much sense to you. However, this is easily remedied. As you read, keep a pad, pencil and dictionary next to you. Whenever you hit a word you don't recognize, write it down and look it up immediately. After five minutes of this, stop and use the Instant Replay technique you discovered in the preceding chapter on Ultra-Mnemonics to fix each word firmly in your memory. When you're sure you know them, transfer them into the permanent storage memory banks in your Ultronic Memory House.

A few weeks' practice of these five techniques should produce a dramatic increase in your reading speed.

### How Mario G. Raised Himself
### from Laborer to Foreman

Mario G. really cashed in on Ultra-Readology! For several years he was a laborer on a construction gang. Then he heard about Ultra-Readology, and decided to give it a try. Every day on his lunch hour he practiced increasing his reading speed, and then started to read as much about the construction business as he possibly could. Within a few weeks, he was able to make several extremely helpful suggestions to his boss—suggestions that saved his boss thousands of dollars. Inside of three months, Mario was promoted to Assistant Foreman, and when his boss was promoted a month later (mostly due to Mario's efforts), Mario was advanced to Foreman. But, unlike his boss, Mario is still young—and his career is just starting!

### The Secret of Ultra-Psychonic Implosion

"Well," you say. "All this is fine. You've shown me how to get my way with other people, improve my memory, get more use out of every spare second, read faster and better and things like that. But, in order to get ahead in life, I need something more—a way to get new ideas, new plans, new strategies—a way to make other people really sit up and take notice of me!"

You'll be pleased to hear that Ultra-Psychonics not only has such a way for you, but that it has been tested and proven 1,000 times over.

I call it "Ultra-Psychonic Implosion," and it works like magic to stimulate the creative powers of your mind.

Here's how it works:

1. On a piece of paper, state your problem or need as clearly as possible. For example, you might write: "I need a way to get $3,000 for a new car."

2. Placing the piece of paper before you, use the two-pan method explained in Chapter 1 to stimulate the flow of egons through your mind, while you keep staring at the statement of your problem.

3. After 10 minutes, dry your hands, and on a separate piece of paper, start to write every thought that has come into your head, no matter how silly it may sound. Your list might look like this:

(1) Lend old car to neighbors, charge $1 a trip.

(2) See if rich uncle Pete will lend me money.

(3) Borrow $500 from six different banks.

(4) Get a regular auto loan.

(5) Have a garage sale to raise money.

(6) Get part-time job on weekends.

(7) Collect old newspapers—sell them to junk dealer.

(8) Start car pool at work; charge passengers.

(9) See if old car can be sold privately for more than book value.

(10) Check into discount store auto sales for lowest price.

Some of these ideas are obviously impractical, some are just ordinary and some are quite new. The important thing to remember when you use this technique is that the new ideas will not come unless you write down *everything* that comes into your head.

### How Helen T. Became a Successful Artist

Helen T., a widow with children to support, was really strapped for cash when she tried this technique. She needed money to support her family, yet her children were so small that she couldn't take an outside job. Using Psychonic Implosion, she quickly determined that her best opportunity was to make use of her artistic talents. She soon found, however, that art is a hard talent to market. There's very little money in trying to sell paintings, unless you have a big reputation, she discovered.

Once again she had a Psychonic Implosion session with herself, and turned up much more practical ways to make her talents pay off. Switching to commercial art, she found that she could sell ideas for greeting cards, cartoons, bookjacket designs and a host of similar items. She now has an income of over $15,000, and never sets her foot outside of her home, except to take her children on vacation trips.

### Advanced Implosion: The Paper Computer Technique

A more sophisticated form of Psychonic Implosion uses a "paper computer" that actually multiplies your brainpower more than 1,000 times. Here is how you use it:

1. Gather together all available materials concerning your problem, and make a list of every related factor you can

think of, regardless of its importance. For example, suppose you want to work out ways of improving your relationships with other people. You would list the things you want to accomplish, such as "cutting down on family arguments" or "getting more friends," and so on.

2. Type or write each entry on your list on a separate card measuring about 2½x3 inches. (Ordinary 3x5 white file cards, cut in half, are just the right size.) One card might read, for example, "Learn new dance steps." Another might say, "Improve memory with Ultra-Mnemonics."

3. Lay the cards out on a table in groups of 12, in no particular order. Each group should be three cards wide by four cards high, with about 1/2 inch between the rows of cards, and about 1 inch between groups of cards.

4. Read over all the cards four or five times, as rapidly as possible, using your new Ultra-Readology skills. This transfers the ideas into your Ultronic Memory House, and starts the Psychonic Implosion process.

5. Do something else in a different room for the next 30 minutes, so that your mind will be occupied completely. You might read a newspaper, or watch TV. While your conscious mind is busy with this activity, your Ultronic Memory House has begun a sorting operation. And because your conscious mind is not interfering, the sorting operation is being carried on at peak efficiency.

6. After 30 minutes, return to the cards. You will notice that now some of them seem to be "friendly" to one another—that is, they seem to fall into the same general category. For example, you now see a connection between "Getting to know more people" and "Improve memory with Ultra-Mnemonics." Collect all the cards into "friendly" groups of this type.

7. Depending on how many cards you started with, you should have several such groups. Put a rubber band around each group. On top of each group, under the rubber band, put a card with a general title that describes all the cards in the group. For example, "have less family arguments" and "don't fight with people at work" might be combined under the general heading of "avoiding arguments."

8. Now do the same thing with each group—combine them into "friendly" batches until you have things reduced to four main batches. These final four groups are the fundamental dimensions of your problem. They are called the "Psychonic Parameters." You might use titles like "Objectives," "Methods," "Areas" and "Persons" to describe the four batches you now have.

9. Next, take one batch, and rearrange its cards into *exactly* six subgroups. These subgroups are called "Ultronic Components." To do this easily, combine the items that are most alike.

10. Type or write the "Psychonic Parameters" and their "Ultronic Components" into four columns, as shown below:

| PSYCHONIC PARAMETER #1 | PSYCHONIC PARAMETER #2 | PSYCHONIC PARAMETER #3 | PSYCHONIC PARAMETER #4 |
|---|---|---|---|
| OBJECTIVES | METHODS | AREAS | PERSONS |
| Have more friends | Better memory | Home | Family |
| Avoid arguments | Increased social life | Work | Fellow workers |
| Make people do what you want | More education | Community activities | Neighbors |
| Prevent others from using you | Improved personal appearance | Parties | Friends |
| Handle difficult people | Improved ability to converse | School | Enemies |
| Appeal more to opposite sex | Knowledge of psychology | Travel | Strangers |

11. Cut up this device, which is called the "Psychonic Imploder," into four vertical strips. (*Important*: Do not cut up the one in the book, as you will not be able to read the next page. Cut up the one you have made yourself.) Each strip should consist of one "Psychonic Parameter" and its six "Ultronic Components."

12. Lay the four strips side by side and slowly move each strip up and down. Note the changing relationships and the new solutions they suggest. Your original 24 "Ultronic Components" have now become 1,296 *combination*

ideas. You have just multiplied your brainpower by more than 1,000 times!

13. To select the best of these 1,296 combination ideas, list them all on several sheets of paper, and go over them carefully. Delete the ones that do not apply to you. For example, if you have no contact with a school situation, cross off all the ones that contain it. Then eliminate the ones that would involve resources that you do not have, or do not want to invest . . . for example, things that cost a lot of money, or that take a long time to accomplish.

14. Eventually, you will find that you have reduced the list down to a dozen or so suggestions—and your problem is solved. At this point, you'll find that the right answer or answers literally leap out at you!

## How Tom E. Made Over $1,000,000 with Two Pieces of Wire

A famous inventor of the past used a method very similar to this in his work. I refer, of course, to the great Thomas Alva Edison.

The story is told that, while he was searching for a suitable filament for the electric light, he tried over 10,000 different substances that did not produce the results he wanted.

"Mr. Edison," someone asked, "don't you feel that you have wasted a lot of time and money on this foolishness?"

"Not at all," he replied, "I have discovered 10,000 things that won't work."

As you know, he eventually did find a substance that worked, and when this substance was placed between two pieces of wire, the first workable electric light was produced. Needless to say, Edison made many millions of dollars from this one invention.

You can see all the elements of Psychonic Implosion in Edison's approach to inventing: the careful assembly of all available information bearing on the problem, the analysis of the problem into its several component parts and the step-by-step testing of every possible solution.

Of course, for most of our problems, we do not have to try every possible alternative. Since we do not face the unknown areas of science, and since in most cases, our resources are fairly limited, we need to try, at most, only a few dozen possibilities.

## Double-Geniology: How to
## Become Twice as Clever

One of the most cherished beliefs that many people have is the idea that they can think of only one thing at a time.

Yet, if you've ever watched a teenager doing his homework while watching TV or listening to the radio, you can quickly see that this is not really the case.

Your mind is not like a piano on which only one person can play at a time, it is more like a symphony orchestra, with many different activities going on simultaneously.

Thus, it is perfectly possible for you to carry on two trains of thought at once. "But," you ask, "why should I?"

The advantages are many. You can get twice as much done in the same amount of time, for example. You can compose a letter to a faraway relative while you also work on your income tax. You can shop for groceries, and plan your next vacation. You can concentrate on doing your morning exercises while you also concentrate on what you're going to do when you get to work.

That, basically, is the technique called Double-Geniology: training your mind to think of two things at a time.

It is an easy skill to pick up. To train yourself to do it, all you need are two radios or two TV sets. Simply set both on different stations, and listen to both stations simultaneously, until you find you can follow both programs without effort at the same time.

You can try other exercises: adding two different columns of figures simultaneously, writing two letters at once and so on.

The next step is to try to master two different activities at once, such as listening to TV and writing a letter. You'll be amazed at how easy it is.

## How Lloyd E. Outwitted His Crooked Partner

Lloyd E. found Double-Geniology particularly useful when he started to suspect that his partner in his restaurant business was cheating him. No matter how hard he worked or how full the restaurant was, the books never seemed to show much profit. The problem in checking things out was that Lloyd was so busy all day he couldn't manage to keep track of everything his partner was doing.

Once Lloyd discovered Double-Geniology, things started to

change. Whenever his partner rang up a sale on the cash register, Lloyd went by and made a mental note of the amount. Using Double-Geniology, he even managed to keep a running total of his own and his partner's sales. At the end of the day, he was surprised to discover that the day's receipts being entered in the books were for a much lower figure. A few more days of checking, and Lloyd called in the police.

They nabbed his partner, and eventually sent him to prison. Meanwhile, Lloyd had his lawyer dissolve the partnership and then repurchased the business for practically nothing. Today he's making a fortune out of the place—but with hired help.

"What a difference!" Lloyd told me. "Two years ago, I was driving a Volkswagen and worrying about paying the rent. Today I own a Cadillac, have a big house in the country all paid off and live like a king!"

### Super-Geniologic: The Great Secret of Network Brain Power

Of course, it is possible to think of more than two things at one time. Most people, with a little practice, can carry on at least four or five trains of thought simultaneously.

The technique for developing this talent is exactly the same as it is for Double-Geniologic. Once you have mastered Double-Geniologic, you can expand it by practicing it while you bring in a third mental focussing point. For example, you can try listening to two radio stations and watching TV. And you can keep expanding your thought channels by adding in other activities, one at a time, until you reach your limit.

Your limit may surprise you. Some people can carry on as many as 12 separate thought streams!

As your mental powers start to increase, you'll notice another phenomenon: *crossover*. What this means is that you'll discover that information from one thought stream is occasionally moving into another, and giving you unexpected help.

For example, suppose you have three thought streams going on simultaneously: #1 is about your job and the people you work with. #2 deals with details of your forthcoming vacation trip to Mexico. #3 concerns your plans for getting money to buy a house. Suddenly, you feel ideas flow from one stream to another: perhaps you can find something in Mexico you can import into the U.S., and make a profit. Another trickle: perhaps someone at work has already been to Mexico and can tell you the best places to go. Another: you recall that your company used to have a policy of lending money to employees to buy homes with. Is it still in effect?

Naturally, the more thought streams you have going, the greater the amount of *crossover*. Here's what the situation looks like, for example, with five thought streams in action:

```
#1 - JOB ———————————————————————————————————————
              |      |                   |
#2 - TRIP ————————————————————————————————————————
                   |              |              |
#3 - HOUSE ———————————————————————————————————————
                        |         |
#4 - ROMANCE ——————————————————————————————————————
                   |              |              |
#5 - AUTO ————————————————————————————————————————
```

As you can see, *crossover* can occur between more than one stream of thought at a time.

With a little practice, you will be able to generate *crossover* whenever you want, instead of just waiting for it to happen. Once you do this, your entire brain becomes a giant network of interlinked thought streams. No matter how many trains of thought you're holding, you now have the ability to flash from one to another at will, connecting one or more for a steady stream of ideas, plans, techniques and strategies for accomplishing any goal.

This is the Great Secret of Network Brain Power. Once you master it, there is literally nothing you cannot do. Your entire brain becomes a mighty machine throbbing with energy, flashing with *crossover* lines and surging forward with multiple streams of thought in a pulsating network of power!

Can it really be done? Certainly! There are chess players, for example, who are able to play 20 or 30 opponents simultaneously. And I'm sure you've heard of Bobby Riggs, the tennis player who is so good that he was able to defeat scores of opponents while he handicapped himself by carrying on a variety of other activities during the game. (Of course, when he ran into Billy Jean King, that was another story. But she was simply a better tennis player, not a better multiple-thinker.)

### How Jerome C. Rose from Rags to Riches

Perhaps the best example of how Network Thinking can turn

the tide in a man's life is the story of Jerome C., a poor immigrant. In just a few years, he started a successful small company in one of the nation's major industries. Then, step-by-step, he expanded his holdings through an enormously complicated setup of interlocking boards of directors, partially owned subsidiaries, conglomerates and holding companies—a system so complex that even the U.S. government couldn't figure it out. By the time he was 60 Jerome C. was a millionaire many times over.

### The Ultimate Secret of Ultra-Geniology: The Mental Organon

"Is it possible to go beyond Network Thinking?" you ask.

Yes, there is one final step: The Mental Organon.

Just as the Psychonic Memory Sphere expanded the capacity of your memory storage banks into four dimensions, so does the Mental Organon expand your thought networks.

Instead of being limited to four or eight or 12 thought streams, your mind can hold as many as 60 or 90 or even more. Things that formerly seemed difficult become mere child's play. Obstacles seem to melt away at a glance. You can even, if you want to, acquire the equivalent of a college education in 10 minutes or less.

To achieve this, study the diagram of the four-dimensional sphere in the chapter on Ultra-Mnemonics. Try to get the "feel" of 4-D space, the visualization of that extra dimension that exists at right angles to our normal 3-D world.

Then, imagine that your thought streams are extending into it. Suddenly, your mind seems to enlarge and there is double the room there was before. You find you have room for many, many more thought streams—and opportunities for an enormously greater number of crossovers. This titanic mental hypersphere is the Mental Organon.

Admittedly, it is a bit difficult to do this. In fact, not everyone can. But a surprising number of people can accomplish it if they are only willing to make the effort. It may take days, perhaps weeks or even longer. No matter how long it takes, it pays for itself 1,000 times over once you achieve it!

## THE MENTAL ORGANON

### The Six-Fold Path to Total Mental Control

This chapter, and the preceding one, have outlined the six basic techniques for total mental control:

1. The Instant Replay technique for quickly memorizing large amounts of data.
2. The Ultronic Memory House for sorting and storing this data.
3. Ultra-Readology for increasing your reading speed.
4. The technique for invoking the Psychonic Image to solve any problems you may face.
5. Ultra-Psychonic Implosion, for creating new ideas.
6. Network Thinking, for multiple brain power.

If you really want to get the maximum out of this book, make every possible effort to master these six techniques. They will truly revolutionize your life, and give you a wonderful new future beyond your wildest imaginings.

### Unlimited Brainpower Multiplication

Is there anything beyond the Psychonic Memory Sphere and the Mental Organon?

Perhaps. But whether anyone is able to achieve it or not is an entirely different question. Every so often, the human race brings forth a rare genius who exceeds the limits of anything that has ever been done before. For such people, the quest for unlimited brain power may just be beginning.

But for most of us, the Six-Fold Path to Total Mental Control will bring us as close to unlimited brainpower multiplication as we will ever want to get.

## WHAT ULTRA-GENIOLOGY CAN DO FOR YOU

In this chapter, we've seen:

- How to put together the bits and pieces of Interstitial Time, and have extra minutes, hours and days to do the things you want.

- How to count on your fingers to over 1,000.

- How to solve problems quickly and easily by making a Psychonic Image model of them.

- How to use five techniques of Ultra-Readology to increase your reading speed by a factor of five or more.

- How to create a roaring storm of new ideas, new strategies, new plans and new techniques with Ultra-Psychonic Implosion and the advanced "paper computer" system.

- How to carry on two or more trains of thought in your mind simultaneously, and link them with the *crossover* network.

- How to expand your mind into four dimensions with the Mental Organon.

This chapter is the heart of the entire system of Ultra-Psychonics. Read it and practice it, over and over, until you have made it your own. Within a very few days, you'll see the results—and they will delight you!

# 6

## ULTRA-EGONICS:
## How to Have
## Better Health, More Vitality
## and a Longer Life

For years, you've probably heard about the virtues of this diet and that diet, this food and that food, this medicine and that medicine, and so on. A few years later, a new diet, food or medicine seems to come along...and the one the authorities used to recommend is suddenly "no good."

If you're tired of this medical version of the old game of musical chairs, Ultra-Egonics may have the answers you're looking for. Instead of a crazy patch-quilt of theories, half-truths and wild guesses, the basic principle of Ultra-Egonics rests on one simple truth: *All pain and illness is caused by interruption of the egonic flow.*

Anyone can see from this that if you restore the egonic flow, the ailment is eliminated. And that's exactly how it works.

### How Ultra-Egonics Has Been Used
### for Centuries Under Other Names

Now I'm not saying that some of the methods that

restore the egonic flow are brand new. On the contrary, many of them have been tested and perfected for thousands of years.

Take Yoga, for example. The basic principles of Yoga were discovered thousands of years ago by the ancient Hindus. Unfortunately, over the centuries, the great basic discovery has been elaborated into such a mish-mash of weird theories, strange contortions and complicated exercises that the original health secret is virtually buried in it, like one raisin in a whole loaf of bread. Yet the one "raisin"—the one fundamental health builder— is what makes the whole thing work.

In this book, I have stripped away the accumulation of nonsense and gibberish that has kept the accumulated health wisdom of the centuries from being used properly, and presented what I believe are the fundamental truths, in terms of Ultra-Egonics.

### The Amazing Growth Force of Ultra-Mitogenic Rays

It is my belief that once you relieve and restore the egonic flow, illness is cured and pain goes away.

Furthermore, sometimes only the simplest methods are needed to do this. Even a rhythmic chant can be effective in some cases. Others may require a simple muscle stretch, or perhaps just the application of plain water in various ways.

Naturally, the more serious the illness, the greater is the interruption of the egonic flow, and the more complex the treatment that is needed.

But the treatment need not be very complicated in many cases. For example, consider these three items that were published recently:

- A congregation in the Midwest prayed over a cornfield every day for a month. Result: the corn in that field grew *75 times faster* than the corn in neighboring fields.

- A boy who was born with a piece of bone missing from his leg was treated by a doctor who simply attached one electric wire on either side of the gap, and ran a small current through it. Result: the bone grew in just a few months, and the boy's leg was whole!

- A woman who had been racked by pain from arthritis all her life went to see one of the new acupuncture doctors. He inserted one small needle into a certain spot, twirled it a few times—and the woman got up and walked, free from pain, for the first time in years!

This is Ultra-Egonics in action!

Is there scientific evidence that egonic flow actually exists? It all depends on how you interpret the evidence. For example, a few decades ago a Russian biologist, Dr. Gurwitch, detected a strange type of radiation being emitted by the roots of newly sprouted onions. This radiation seemed to stimulate cell activity in general, and actually produced a rejuvenating effect on certain life forms. There are many different interpretations of this phenomenon—but it is my belief that these onion roots were emitting "ultra-mitogenic rays"—and that these rays increased the egonic flow in living beings by affecting the conductivity of the cells, just as lowering the temperature of a copper wire increases its ability to conduct electricity.

## The Secret of Ultra-Yoga

What is the basic discovery that the ancient Hindus made so many thousands of years ago? It is simply this: in order to control the workings of your body, *you must learn to relax.*

I'm not talking about sitting down in an easy chair and just slumping down. I'm talking about relaxing every nerve, muscle and fiber of your body so that you can command and control it.

Try this Ultra-Yoga ritual:

1. Lie down on the floor, and loosen any tight belts or other close-fitting garments you may be wearing. Now, deliberately tighten up every muscle in your body: clench your fists, stiffen your arms and legs, pull in your stomach, clench your teeth, arch your toes. Hold this position for a few seconds. Now, starting with your toes, slowly release the tension. Let them go limp. Next, let a slow wave of limpness start to move up your legs, and then up your body. Relax your arms, your wrists, your fingers. Unclench your teeth. And so on, until you have relaxed every part of your body. Feel the tension flow out of you. For the first time in your life, you are enjoying complete relaxation. Enjoy the sensation for five minutes. Then, tense yourself up again, and repeat the whole process. Repeat this again three more times. Stop for the day.

2. Repeat the entire five sets of five-minute relaxation once a day for a week. Feel how the tension and stress is starting to leave your body.

3. Repeat as often as necessary, until you feel completely calm and at your ease. If you have a particularly trying day, repeat the relaxation ritual just before you go to bed.

"But," you ask, "what about all the rest of that Yoga stuff—the breathing exercises, the arm and leg positions, the standing on the head?"

You are right. Traditional Yoga goes far beyond this basic relaxation secret, and those who are willing to spend months and years to master it can often perform remarkable physical feats. But Ultra-Yoga is not aimed at such acrobatic goals. It is aimed at restoring your body's egonic flow, to bring you better health.

### How Wanda C. Overcame Her Insomnia

I'm sure Wanda C. would agree with me. I first met her five years ago, and she looked terrible. She had deep, dark, heavy rings under her eyes and moved like a woman 30 years older. Listless, tired, she barely had enough energy to drag herself to work every morning. Her problem was that she couldn't seem to sleep more than four or five hours a night. After talking to her a while, I found out that she was a chronic worrier. She worried about her job, about her boyfriend, about her health—day and night. She didn't believe how easy it was to relax with Ultra-Yoga when I told her about it, but she said she'd try it anyway. Within a week, the change was astonishing. Her insomnia vanished, the bags started to disappear from under her eyes, her health improved—and she started to look and feel years younger.

The last time I saw her, about a year ago, she was the picture of health— and actually looked 10 years younger than her calendar age. I've heard that she even does modeling these days.

### A Gypsy Health Secret Revealed

Do gypsies use the health secrets of Ultra-Egonics? It is entirely possible that they do, although any gypsy you meet would probably laugh at the idea.

But take the little-known Gypsy Wake-Up Energizer, for example. It consists of stretching each arm and each leg every morning, *before* you get out of bed. Try it, and you'll discover that you bound out of bed bursting with energy, without any of the usual fuzziness or confusion you usually get when you sit up and put your legs on the floor.

How do you explain this in terms of Ultra-Egonics? Obviously, it is the Ultra-Yoga tense-and-relax ritual being repeated here. Just as the starter button of an automobile starts the motor turning over smoothly, so that it can start running on its own, so does the Gypsy Wake-Up Energizer ritual bring your body's egonic flow up to full power in the morning.

## How Bernard H. Became More Alert and Vigorous

Bernard H., who I met a few months ago, also suffered from insomnia, although not as badly as Wanda did. But in his case, it was a lot more dangerous. Every morning he would stumble out of bed bleary-eyed and tired, hack up his face trying to shave and then go to work. He was a cab driver. You can well imagine what his day was like—a nightmarish series of missed lights, close brushes with accidents, meandering trips that annoyed his riders and cut down his tips and the like. The only reason he even had a job was that he owned his own cab.

I suggested that he try both the Ultra-Yoga relaxation ritual at night and the Gypsy Wake-Up Energizer in the morning. Since he was facing the loss of his license by the Taxi Bureau, he decided he'd give it a whirl.

In just a few weeks, things started to change. Bernard found he had almost more energy than he knew what to do with. His driving record improved, he looked and felt better and even his income started to grow. It's been like watching a dried stick come to life in the spring time, and put forth leaves and blossoms. For the first time in years, he has a girlfriend, money in the bank and bright prospects.

## Ultra-Egonic Health Chants

Even sound waves can restore the egonic flow under certain conditions, especially when the cause of the blockage is of a similar nature.

Today, for example, doctors often use hypnotism to cure certain nervous conditions. This is nothing new, of course. For centuries, wizards, witchdoctors and medicine men cured patients by mystic chants and magic health songs. Naturally, it didn't work in many cases—but where psychonic factors were involved, it used to perform amazing miracles of healing.

How can we adapt this technique to the modern world?

Obviously, we want to dispense with the turkey feather headdresses and the snakeskin rattles. But what remains?

Sound. Words strung together in natural rhythmic groups that help to restore the body's natural egonic flow. Let us call them Ultra-Egonic Health Chants.

Even the words are not important. It is the *vibrations* that count. There is an ancient magic word used in the Orient—"OM"—which is said to have remarkable powers. Try it. Say "OM" slowly, over and over, making it rhyme with "home." After you have said this word four or five times, you will feel the vibration from it starting to build up in your body, getting stronger and stronger.

These vibrations can actually unblock certain types of egonic flow. You can feel it happening. You can see why the ancient healers who knew this secret were considered to be wizards and magicians.

Or take the "A" sound. You've probably heard stage-magicians say "Abra-Cadabra!" Yet this word goes way back—it was once used for real magical purposes, and was carved as a Word of Power on magical talismans and amulets. Why? Try repeating it slowly, over and over. Feel the vibrations surge through your body.

Perhaps that is why the main god of the ancient Egyptians was named "Ra." Imagine thousands of people chanting this sound over and over, until the very ground trembled!

Here are five Ultra-Egonic Health Chants. Try them when you feel ill at ease, when you're a little under the weather and don't know what's bothering you or when you have what some people call the "blahs": (Repeat each chant for exactly 60 seconds, slowly.)

1. Home-home-home home-home-home
   Home-home-home home-home-home

2. Knee-knee-knee-knee knee-knee-knee-knee
   Knee-knee-knee-knee knee-knee-knee-knee

3. Ra-ra ra-ra ra-ra ra
   Abra-cadabra Abra-cadabra
   Ra-ra ra

4. None-none none-none none-none none
   None none-none-none none
   None-none none

5. High-high high-ha
   High-high ha
   High-high high-ha
   High-high ha

Note exactly which chant made you feel better. Then repeat it, over and over for five minutes. Rest for 30 seconds. Repeat for another five minutes. Continue doing this until you feel relief from whatever is bothering you. Remember that each word must be pronounced *slowly*, until you can feel the vibration from it.

## How Sarah Z. Overcame a Disfiguring Skin Condition

A young girl I knew a few years ago found these Health Chants extremely effective in clearing up a bad case of pimples. Sarah Z.'s pimples were so bad that she not only had no boyfriends, she even had trouble finding a job. She had been to several doctors, but their treatments did not help her, as the pimples were caused by a nervous condition.

Once she tried the Health Chants, she found that Nos. 2 and 4 had a strange, soothing effect on her, especially when she chanted them very slowly. Within two days, her pimples started to disappear, as a result of her being more relaxed and at ease, and within three weeks they were all gone!

## Ultra-Oculism

Is poor eyesight caused by blockages in the egonic flow?

I believe this may definitely be the case in many instances, and a technique exists for correcting the problem.

Actually, this technique—called "palming"—was developed independently of Ultra-Psychonics by the well-known Dr. Bates. However, most explanations of why it works are not very satisfactory. If you apply the basic principles of Ultra-Egonics to it, on the other hand, its mechanism becomes considerably clearer and more understandable.

Here is how it works: Remove your glasses. Next, place one hand over each eye, with the fingers crossing over the top of your nose. Close your eyes. Now open them in the dark and keep them open for a few minutes. Take away your hands. See how much better your eyes feel. If you test them, you will find that you can actually see a little better than you did before. If you continue to use this technique over a long period of time, dramatic improvement in your eyesight is possible, according to Dr. Bates.

In terms of Ultra-Egonics, crossing your fingers connects them into a circuit. Thus, a series of new pathways is created, and the egonic flow around your eyes is considerably altered. If the cause of your poor eyesight was an egonic blockage, the egons are now able to flow around the barrier and deliver their health-producing energies directly to the eyes. Continued use of the technique, of course, not only helps the eyes, but also helps to dissolve the original barriers, since they are bombarded by egons on both sides, instead of just one. Rubbing the palms together briskly before palming can intensify the effect, by increasing the egonic charge on the hands.

### How Fred D. Improved His Eyesight and Threw Away His Glasses

Does the "palming" technique really work? There are some unusual cases on record, including an Englishman who palmed his eyes continuously for an entire day—and found his eyes had improved from 20/400 to 20/200 overnight.

However, I can state positively that I have seen this technique work in at least two cases.

In one of them, the gradual loss of eyesight was halted, and, while the person's eyes did not improve, he was able to use the same pair of glasses for over ten years.

The other case, Fred D., is somewhat more dramatic. Fred D. got such excellent results from palming that within one month he literally threw away his eyeglasses, and has never had to use them since. "It was a little hard at first," he told me, "but my eyesight has now returned completely to normal."

### Ultra-Thermodynamics

Another method of releasing a blocked-up egonic flow is the application of temperature variation to the afflicted area. Both heat and cold are helpful, and in some cases alternation of the two gives the best results.

A friend of mine, for example, fell down a flight of stairs some months ago, and badly sprained both ankles. Instead of calling a doctor, his wife decided to treat the ankles herself. She bought four large icebags at her local drugstore, and kept at least one on each of her husband's ankles at all times. The other two were kept in reserve, so that there would not be a break in the cold.

Not only did her husband find that the pain was diminished to practically nothing, but after one day, he found that he was 90% better. By the end of the second day, he was able to walk around without any pain at all, and by the end of the third day, he was able to return to work, feeling completely cured.

There were no relapses, no side-effects, no complications—and the only cost was for the icebags.

If you use this method, and the person being treated finds that the cold becomes unbearable, it is safe to take the icebags away for a half hour or so every few hours.

Another example of the method's effectiveness is from my own life. Some years ago, I accidentally rammed the outside of my thigh into the edge of a metal desk drawer. Shortly thereafter, I started to get terrible shooting pains up and down the entire leg. I immediately applied the principles of Ultra-Thermodynamics. At 15-minute intervals, for several hours, I alternated an icebag with an electric heating pad against the painfully throbbing thigh. The pain stopped in less than an hour, and by that evening the entire thigh felt as though it was as good as new. I thought the pain might recur the next day, but it didn't—and the thigh has never bothered me again.

### How Adrian F. Overcame a Lifelong Stomach Problem

An acquaintance of mine, Adrian F., used Ultra-Thermodynamics to overcome a lifetime problem he had had with a "nervous stomach." He had been using a hot water bottle for many years to relieve the worst of his pains. He decided to apply Ultra-Thermodynamic techniques to see if they could help him get rid of the condition permanently.

I had told him of my experience in getting rid of the pain in my thigh, and he decided to try a similar method. Each evening he waited at least two hours for his dinner to digest, and then got into a warm bed. He then alternated a hot water bottle and an icebag, each for a half hour. Then he turned out the light and went to sleep.

After a week of this, he found there was a remarkable improvement in his condition. No longer was he suddenly seized by terrible chills and excruciating pains in his stomach during moments of stress on his job. Even when his boss yelled at him—and his boss yelled at everyone quite often—he no longer felt as though his stomach was twisting itself into a knot. His work improved very dramatically, and he soon received a substantial raise. Furthermore, his boss no longer picked on him, since he became one of his department's top producers.

Adrian's stomach problem still recurs—but only on very rare occasions. He now finds that just one evening of treatment will stop it instantly, and it won't bother him again for six months or more.

### Ultra-Hydrodynamics

Perhaps you're wondering what happens when you combine the vibratory power of the Health Chants with the temperature variations of Ultra-Thermodynamics. The result is Ultra-Hydrodynamics—the amazing technique of healing with water!

Here's how it works: a stream of either hot or cold water is sprayed directly on the afflicted part for exactly three minutes. Then the water is towelled-off briskly, the body rested for another three minutes and the entire process repeated. Generally speaking, cold water is more effective than hot water. However, when hot water sprays are alternated with cold water sprays, the effects are better than when just one or the other is used.

All that is needed for the spray is an ordinary spray hose of the type sold in houseware stores. The best place to spray is, of course, in the bathtub.

In one instance, a long-lasting cough was broken up simply by letting the spray from a regular shower beat upon the throat and upper chest for five minutes every morning, followed by the normal cleansing of the body in the shower. The cough disappeared in three days.

Care should be taken not to make the water too hot for the hot water spray. Ordinary bath temperature is the best—warm enough to feel pleasant, but not hot enough to scald yourself.

For situations where a part of the body is bruised—such as a finger bruised by a window slamming on it, or a blister on the palm—it is better to use cold water exclusively. The part should be sprayed until it is slightly numbed, and then allowed to return to room temperature without being rubbed or towelled. The process should be repeated for at least an hour three times a day.

It is also possible to rid yourself of warts this way. A steady stream of cold water on the wart for five minutes a day will cause it to shrivel up and fall off in a surprisingly short time—sometimes in as little as a week.

### How Farmer John J. Rid Himself of Persistent
### Backache with a Special Ultra-Hydrodynamic Water Bath

An acquaintance of mine, who worked on a farm, complained to me that he had excruciatingly painful backaches almost every night due to the heavy physical nature of his work.

He tried his own version of Ultra-Hydrodynamics, as follows: He filled the bottom of his bathtub with about 3 or 4 inches of warm water, and lay in it for five minutes. Then he let the water out and replaced it with the same amount of cold water. He continued alternating the hot and cold water for about two hours.

When he finally stopped, he towelled himself down thoroughly and went right to bed. In the morning his backache was completely gone and has never returned.

### How Teacher Lorraine I. Cured
### Her Daily Headaches

After a hard day in the classroom, Lorraine I. went home with a splitting headache every night. She, too, tried Ultra-Hydrodynamics in the form of a gentle facial spray over the sink, as soon as she got home each day. She found that alternating warm and cold sprays gave her the best results. Not only did her headaches cease, but she discovered that she was filled with energy for the rest of the evening instead of being all tired out.

### Ultra-Nutrition

There are, of course, certain types of food that also help to restore the egonic flow. It is hard to say exactly why—they just seem to have some quality about them that stimulates the body. Here are some of them:

GARLIC: A housewife I know had a steady pain in her ear for many months. She went to several doctors without result, including an ear specialist. Finally, she tried keeping a clove of garlic in her mouth for several hours a day. She felt better almost immediately, and after four days, she felt something "pop" in her ear. The pain vanished and it has never bothered her again.

YOGURT/WHEAT GERM: This should be eaten every morning. Use about one tablespoon of wheat germ to a cup of yogurt. The yogurt can either be plain or flavored. In the winter, use two or three tablespoons of wheat germ. Several people I know do this, and report that it not only fills them with tremendous energy every morning, but that in the winter, it keeps them so warm that they can barely stand to wear a coat. None of them have had a cold for years.

ONION SOUP: Another wonder-working food seems to be onion soup. You recall that earlier in this chapter we talked about the work of Dr. Gurwitch with "ultra-mitogenic" rays, based on his experiments with onions. Whether these rays are involved or not, there certainly seems to be tremendous healing power in onion soup. A young executive I know threw off a bad case of the flu in less than a week, without bothering to go see a doctor. He ate hot onion soup three or four times a day, and said it was better than penicillin.

OTHER EGONIC FOODS: Several other foods also seem to be effective in restoring the egonic flow: bananas, liver, spinach, honey, apples and cranberry juice. They seem to have a very beneficial effect on the body, and relieve many minor ailments. Cranberry juice, for example, does wonders in relieving irritations of the urinary tract. And, to paraphrase an old proverb, "a banana a day keeps stomachaches away."

### How Weak, Listless Tim K.
### Became a Top Athlete

The power of these "food medicines" is demonstrated by the effect they had on a young man I know named Tim K. Tim was truly a "97-pound weakling," and, although he tried to build up his muscles, he never seemed to get anywhere. After incorporating several egonic foods into his diet, particularly spinach and liver, a miracle occurred. Tim suddenly filled out to his normal weight, and his muscle-building exercises immediately started to work for him. In just a few months, he had the rippling muscles and powerful physique that he'd always wanted. Where girls had laughed at him before, now they flock to him like bees to honey. He's a very happy fellow these days.

If you want more pep and energy, more strength and endurance, try these egonic foods for a month, and see what happens!

### The Secret of Egonic Herbs

The value of herbs has been proven for many thousands of years. However, some herbs seem to work better than others in restoring certain types of egonic flow. For example:

COMFREY: This is easily obtained at any health food store. The roots are more effective than the leaves, although both have considerable healing power. The best way to take comfrey is in the form of a cup of tea, with honey. You can use comfrey teabags, or loose comfrey, whichever you prefer. Pour boiling water over the teabag, or over one tablespoonful of the loose herb, and let it stand for about five minutes. Comfrey has been reported as an effective remedy for a wide variety of ailments, including coughs, stomach conditions, kidney trouble, anemia and diarrhea.

FENNEL: This herb can be found in the spice rack in your local grocery or supermarket, and can also be obtained in teabag and loose form at health stores. Prepare it as a tea, with honey, in the same manner as comfrey. This herb is particularly effective in breaking up long-lasting coughs, and has been used in Europe for this purpose for many centuries.

GINSENG: This herb, which was known to the Chinese as early as 3000 B.C., is regarded as the highest and most potent of their herbs. The great Chinese herb expert Shen-ung claims that ginseng is "a tonic to the five major organs: the brain, lungs, heart, stomach and intestines" and that, if taken for some time, "will invigorate the body and prolong life." Ginseng, which is usually taken in tea form, unfortunately is somewhat expensive, although it can easily be obtained at health food stores.

For more information about these, and other herbs, I suggest you read, *Nature's Medicines* by Richard Lucas (Parker Publishing Co.), *Modern Encyclopedia of Herbs* by Joseph M. Kadans (Parker Publishing Co.) and *The Herb Buyer's Guide* by Richard Heffern (Pyramid Books).

### How Ida E. Speeded Her Recovery from Pneumonia

The kind of help these egonic herbs can provide is best illustrated by the case of Ida E., a retired teacher whom I know. Last winter, Ida was stricken by a bad case of pneumonia, and although she went to see a doctor and was "cured" by antibiotics, she just couldn't seem to get her strength back. Months passed, and she was still as weak as a kitten. Then I suggested comfrey tea to her, and she started to drink it three times a day. In just three days, she started to feel better, and by the end of the week, she told me, "I think all the poison is starting to wash out of my system."

One month later, when she went for a checkup, the doctor told her that her lungs were perfectly clear, and a test of her breathing capacity showed that it was now completely normal.

### How Li Chung Yun Lived to the Age of 256 Years

Another unusual egonic herb is Fo-ti-Tieng, obtainable only in health food stores. A famous Chinese herbalist, Li Chung Yun, was reported by *The New York Times* to have lived to the age of 256. At the age of 200, he gave a course of 28 lectures on longevity at a Chinese university, and those who saw him said that he did not appear older than a man of 52, that he stood straight and strong and that he still had his natural hair and teeth.

He regularly used two herbs in tea form, Fo-ti-Tieng and ginseng, and with the exception of the ginseng root, would eat only food that was produced above the ground.

Considering the primitive state of the medical arts during most of Li Chung Yun's lifetime, who knows how long he might have lived if he had been born in the Twentieth Century? The average lifespan for an American born in the Nineteenth Century never rose to more than 48—today, it is over 75, an increase of almost 60%!

## Ultra-Vitamins

Most people have heard of Vitamins A, B, C, D and E—but did you know there are at least half a dozen others. All vitamins, of course, stimulate and strengthen the egonic flow, but perhaps some of the less well-known ones may be missing from your diet:

VITAMIN F: Lack of this vitamin can produce emaciation, severe skin rashes, kidney disorders, slow healing of even small wounds, poor fertility and shortening of the life span. Good sources of this vitamin are peanut oil, olive oil, butter, cream, egg yolk, avocado and fish-liver oil.

VITAMIN G: This vitamin is especially valuable in combination with Vitamin A for prevention and correction of cataracts, and for health of skin, hair and eyes. Glandular meats, such as that of the heart, liver or kidney are high in this vitamin, and it is also found in broccoli, lettuce, cabbage and wheat germ.

VITAMIN H: A deficiency of this vitamin may cause loss of appetite, nausea, low-grade anemia, intense depression, insomnia and muscle pains. Best sources of this vitamin are egg yolks, liver and yeast.

VITAMIN K: This vitamin helps the blood clot faster, and prevents hemorrhages. Other conditions caused by the lack of Vitamin K are fatigue, general itching and slow heart action. The best sources of Vitamin K are leafy green vegetables, especially spinach; as well as rose hips and alfalfa. Yogurt is helpful in aiding the body to produce its own Vitamin K if the intestinal bacteria are weak or sparsely distributed.

VITAMIN P: Deficiency of this vitamin results in tissue swelling, pain in legs, limbs and joints, weakness of muscles and tiredness. It is also used in combination with Vitamin C to cure scurvy. The best source of Vitamin P is paprika juice, but it is also plentiful in most vegetable juices and in lemon rind.

VITAMIN U: This vitamin is presently being investigated as a healing agent in peptic ulcers, and is thought to be the factor responsible for the remarkable cures of stomach ulcers in human patients by medical researchers at Stanford University. The vitamin has also been found effective in treating and preventing high blood pressure. It is present in cabbage juice, and in alfalfa. (Alfalfa for human use is specially prepared and should be purchased in a health food store.)

VITAMIN X: Also known as the "youth vitamin," this is believed to be the active ingredient in the herb Fo-ti-Tieng. A French biochemist who investigated this substance found that it had a rare tonic quality which has a marked energizing effect on nerves and brain cells, and seems to exert a rejuvenating effect on the ductless glands. A 107-year-old Hindu sage, Nanddo Narian, asserts that Fo-ti-Tieng provides a missing ingredient in man's diet, without which he can never wholly control disease and decay. An Indian herb, Gotu Kola, is also said to have the same longevity-producing powers as Fo-ti-Tieng.

## How Louis A. Got Rid of a Persistent Cough

Louis A., a young factory worker, had a persistent cough which he just couldn't seem to get rid of. He had been to several doctors and taken all sorts of antibiotics, but the cough just seemed to hang on.

When I met him, he had had the cough for a year and a half, and was trying massive doses of Vitamin C, without effect. I suggested to him that he add some Vitamin P to his diet, and within a month, his cough had disappeared.

## The Secret of Egonic Awareness

Is it possible to heal yourself from within, purely by the power of your mind? In some cases, the answer is a resounding "Yes!"

I call this technique "egonic awareness"—and here's how it works:

1. Use the Ultra-Yoga ritual explained earlier in this chapter for complete relaxation, lying on the floor.

2. Generate an egonic flow, as explained in Chapter 1, and direct the flow down into your left foot.

3. Next, direct the flow into your smallest toe. Try to feel every part of the inside of your toe: the nail, the flesh and the bone. Feel the egons flowing through each part and returning to your brain. Concentrate on this feeling until you have a mental "blueprint" of every muscle, nerve and tissue in that toe.

4. Now do the same for the next toe.

5. Continue doing this until you have a mental "blueprint" of every part of your foot. Then, do the same thing for the other foot.

6. Next, do your legs, then your fingers and arms.

7. Next, do your main torso, taking it in three sections: first, from your crotch to your navel, then from your navel to the bottom of your ribcage and finally from your ribcage up to your neck. This section is where you will have most of your ailments, so concentrate on complete mastery of every gland, nerve, muscle and organ. (If you are not sure exactly what is in each section, take a look at an anatomy book or one of those plastic models of the human body they sell in hobby stores.)

8. Next, do your neck, and finally, your entire head.

The essence of this technique is to pick one small part of your body at a time, and concentrate on it until its structure, its "blueprint," is locked in the files of your Ultronic Memory House. It is important to repeat this technique over and over until you can touch and feel any part of your body in an instant.

Then, when any part of your body is hurt or doesn't feel well, your "egonic awareness" goes to work for you, and makes the necessary repairs. The mental "blueprint" of your body focuses the egonic flow on the part that doesn't feel right, and concentrates your body's total healing power where it will do the most good.

## WHAT ULTRA-EGONICS CAN DO FOR YOU

In this chapter, you've seen:

- How Ultra-Egonics has been used for centuries under other names.

- How Ultra-Mitogenic rays can increase the egonic flow.

- How Ultra-Yoga can help you control the workings of your body.

- How the Gypsy Wake-Up Energizer can help you start each day filled with vigor and vitality.
- How certain healing sound waves can be focussed with Ultra-Egonic Health Chants.
- How "palming" can help to improve your eyesight.
- How Ultra-Thermodynamics can release a blocked-up egonic flow.
- How plain water can become a powerful tool in your healing arsenal.
- How certain foods can have an almost magical effect on various ailments, due to their egon-stimulating qualities.
- How egonic herbs can work healing miracles.
- How the little-known Ultra-Vitamins can help restore ailing parts of the body, and may have unusual powers of rejuvenation.
- How "egonic awareness" can help your body heal itself from within, without any other medical help.

... and that's only the beginning. Practice the techniques you've discovered in this chapter, read some of the books I've mentioned and conduct your own tests. See how soon these techniques will have you looking better, feeling better and living longer!

# 7

## ULTRA-ASTRONICS:

## How to
## Read the Messages
## in the Sky

There *are* messages in the sky. I'm not talking about skywriting, or radio, or astrology. I'm talking about real messages that can help you find romance, make money, get ahead in business, even have a better vacation.

### Why Old-Fashioned Astrology Is No Longer Accurate

Now, of course, some people will say, "Doesn't astrology do all those things?"

The answer is "yes" and "no." Yes, astrology does seem to help people in some cases—and no, it doesn't really do so.

Many astrological predictions are, oddly enough, self-fulfilling. If you read in the paper that people born under your Zodiac sign should try to avoid arguments the next day, one of two things will happen: you will either avoid argument s or not. If you manage to avoid them, you will breathe a sigh of relief and say, "Thank goodness, I sure saved myself a lot of trouble by following my horoscope." On the other hand, if you have the arguments, you will say, "What can I do? It was fated to happen."

This is not very serious, usually, as long as it is confined to the bland sort of advice usually found in such newspaper columns. On the other hand, it's usually not very helpful either. And when people do start following detailed astrological advice seriously, as Hitler did in World War II, complete disaster can often result.

In addition to this, astrology is a complicated business. It involves a lot of difficult mathematics, if you try to do it yourself. Even if you hire someone, the data is capable of many different interpretations, and there's always the chance that the person you hire will select the one that benefits *him* most.

Why bother with such a chancy, slipshod method when there's something much better available?

It's called Ultra-Astronics.

### The Real Signs in the Sky and What They Mean

The sky is filled with information that can help you, if you know what to look for. There are visible and invisible signs that can predict the future as accurately as a watch tells the time.

The moon, for example, can tell you some amazing things about your friends, co-workers and neighbors. You'll find out very shortly, when you discover the secret of Ultra-Lunology.

And there are more subtle signs: temperature, barometric pressure and ionic charge. They can work miracles for you, if you know how to interpret and apply them to certain situations.

Finally, there is the astounding Psychonic Zodiac. No hanky-panky here—just a simple, logical explanation of why different types of people act the way they do, and how you can use this knowledge to control and manipulate them.

Put all these signs together in the special way you're about to discover, and you can set up your Ultra-Astronic Chart—a chart that lets you predict exactly what other people are going to do just as surely as the sun rises in the morning.

"But," you say, "Zodiacs, charts—it sounds an awful lot like good, old-fashioned astrology. What's the difference?"

The difference, my friend, is that Ultra-Astronics *works every time,* and astrology doesn't. The difference is that Ultra-Astronics is simple and easy to do. And above all, the difference is that there is just *one way* to interpret the results—and the results are guaranteed.

## The New Science of Ultra-Astronics and How It Can Help You

By now, you're probably wondering exactly how Ultra-Astronics can help you in specific ways. Here's just a small sampling of what it can do:

- It can tell you exactly what your chances are of succeeding in any given venture, whether it's asking your boss for a raise, winning a game of tennis, baking a cake or anything else.
- It can let you know when a member of the opposite sex is in the most responsive mood for your advances—and guide you toward doing everything just right, so that he or she will have as wonderful and rewarding an experience as you do.
- It can protect you from saying or doing anything wrong that will turn people against you.
- It can help you make a lot of new friends faster and more easily than you ever thought possible.
- It can tell you which days are the best for making important personal decisions.
- It can reveal which days are ideal for travel, and on which days you should stay at home.
- It can point out which days are best for different types of investment and other financial activities.
- It can warn you which days will be the most dangerous for you, and indicate how you can get through them safely.
- It can let you know when your pets want to be played with, and when it is best to leave them alone.
- It can reveal the times when your creative, artistic and psychic powers are at their maximum each day, so that you can reach new peaks of achievement.

. . . And that's only the beginning!

## How Sidney A. Made His New Restaurant a Success

I recently read of a restaurant owner named Sidney A. who, unknowingly, used the principles of Ultra-Astronics to turn his new restaurant into a rip-roaring success.

His new restaurant was just not catching on. It was in a good location, it was nicely furnished and the food was just as tasty as anything his competitors served. But somehow, there was a shortage of customers.

People would come in, sit around for a while and then just leave after a drink or two. Very few people seemed to want to order a full meal, and those that did never came back.

Sidney was at his wits' end when an accident saved him. His dishwasher accidentally dropped a pot of water and shorted-out the air conditioner. He called an electrician, and when the repair was completed, the man told him, "Your machine is even better than it was before."

"How so?" asked Sidney.

"It wasn't connected up right," said the electrician.

That proved to be a great understatement. Within a week, business started to pick up, and then to boom. By the end of the month, people needed a reservation to get in.

What one change did the electrician make that turned Sidney's failing restaurant into a roaring success?

I'm going to tell you in a little while . . . but first, I want to introduce you to one of the cornerstones of Ultra-Astronics . . . the secret of Ultra-Lunology. It's based on one of the most visible and easily observed signs in the sky . . . the moon itself.

## Ultra-Lunology

The moon . . . ruler of the night. Does it also rule the people under it?

Science says yes. It's a known fact that certain types of mentally-ill people are so strongly affected by the full moon, for example, that they get quite violent when it is in the sky.

But what about normal people? They, too, are affected. Any businessman knows how the flow of customer complaints starts to increase as the moon becomes full, and how it diminishes when the moon is dark.

This is the secret of Ultra-Lunology: that the moon affects all of us, *all the time.* And furthermore, the effect can be measured precisely and scientifically.

Why the moon has this effect is a deep mystery. It is my own belief that the additional light energy reflected by the moon onto the earth and its inhabitants disturbs the egonic flow of the body, in a very subtle way.

As you saw in the preceding chapter, *any* interruption of the egonic flow creates some sort of bodily disturbance. In this case, the change is in the emotional channels.

Observe this for yourself. Consult a calendar that shows the phases of the moon: 1st ¼–Full; 3rd ¼–New.

Make a note of these phases for the coming month. Then pick out someone you know. See how his or her moods change as the various phases of the moon occur. You have made an important discovery about that person—and without their being even aware of it. What's more, you can use this information in a variety of ways.

Suppose this person had been your boss. You would then know when the best time to ask for a raise would be, when to avoid agitating him and when it's best to keep out of his way altogether. You'd know when to convince him and when to agree with him. In short, you'd have a tremendous advantage over him that none of your co-workers would. Think of how this could benefit you!

### How Wallace W. Won the Hand of Sylvia K.

Wallace W., a young lawyer, had been trying to get his girl, Sylvia K., to marry him for several years. No matter what he did, he just couldn't seem to get her to say "yes."

I ran into Wallace on a business deal several years ago, and got to know him quite well. A mutual friend had tipped me off about Wallace's problem, and I decided I would try to help him.

One day, at lunch, I started to talk to him about Ultra-Lunology, without mentioning it by name, or its connection with Ultra-Psychonics. Instead, I spoke of the mysterious psychic changes that occur during the various phases of the moon, and how people's moods can often be predicted by observing how they reacted to each phase.

Wallace, who had been listening at first with an abstracted air, suddenly came to life. "How do you do it?" he asked seriously.

I explained the technique of Ultra-Lunology to him and he listened intently.

About two months later, I received a wedding announcement

from Wallace W. and Sylvia K. They've been happily married ever since.

### Ultra-Ionics

As I promised, I'm going to reveal exactly how Sidney A. saved his failing restaurant business. What happened was that the electrician called in to repair his short-circuited air conditioner noticed that the polarity was reversed, and fixed it simply by switching two wires back the way they were supposed to be.

A minor change? Not exactly, although all it did really was to change the "smell" of the air. But scientists have found that some pretty startling things happen when you do this. Reverse what they call the "ground-to-air-static-charge gradient" and lab animals start to act strangely, even irrationally. Some seem to go berserk. Others simply sit in a state of complete dejection or despair.

Now if this condition only occurred artificially, there would be no problem. But the same situation occurs in nature. If you've ever noticed how jumpy and nervous people get before a storm, you know what I mean. And that's also the reason why so many otherwise normal people become absolutely terrified of thunder and lightning when a storm is going on. You may be one of them yourself.

What can you do about it? Try this Ultra-Ionics technique:

1. Rub the palms of your hands together briskly for about 15 to 20 seconds, until you feel a tingling sensation.

2. Rub each palm against the various parts of your body you can reach, moving them always toward your heart. This is called Egonic Palming.

In a very short time, you will feel the tension and nervousness start to drain away, and you will become completely calm again.

However, the important thing about Ultra-Ionics is not how the electricity in the air affects you, but how it affects others. Once you understand that other people's moods and reactions can be affected by this factor, you have a powerful tool for predicting and controlling their reactions. A little further on in this chapter, you'll see how to use this data to the greatest possible effect.

## How Dave L. Made the Biggest
## Sale of His Career

Dave L. was particularly sensitive to the electric charge in the air, without knowing it. All he knew was that sometimes he was a great salesman, and other times he could barely get his mouth open. A day or two before a storm, he was often so nervous that he would call in sick and stay home from work. Needless to say, his over-all sales record was very poor.

Once he found out about Ultra-Ionics, however, he was a changed man. Whenever he started to feel nervous and jumpy, he used the Egonic Palming technique, and found that in a few minutes, he was back to normal.

Gradually, his confidence—and his sales record—started to build up. In less than three months, he had smashed all his previous sales records, and had made his first $1,000,000 sale—the biggest sale of his career. Shortly after that, he was promoted to sales manager, and his career has been going up steadily ever since.

## Ultra-Barometrics

An effect similar to that of Ultra-Ionics also occurs when the barometric pressure rises and falls. This aspect of Ultra-Astronics is very easy to keep track of—you don't even need a barometer. Simply listen to your local TV weatherman every night, and watch carefully when he points out the highs and lows on the weather map.

Then, as you did in Ultra-Lunology, set up a series of charts on the various people you come in contact with. See how they react to things on the days when the air pressure is high and when it is low. See which days they are more agreeable to suggestion, and which days they tend to resist.

Before you know it, you can start to control and direct their lives and make them do the things you want. Yet all it takes is a few minutes each evening listening to your TV!

Of course, if you want to do things even more scientifically, you can invest a few dollars in your own barometer and find out how to read it. This will give you hour-by-hour data that you can use to even greater effect.

"But," you say, "suppose I am strongly affected by these air-pressure changes myself? How do I overcome this?"

That's a very good question. On analyzing the problem, however, one fact immediately emerges. The barometric reactions are mainly caused by *differences* in air pressure between your body and the surrounding atmosphere.

Thus, simply taking deep breaths for two or three minutes before you are about to have an important personal contact will help equalize the pressure and help put you in a completely relaxed and energetic frame of mind. This is called BPR breathing, since it gives your body a Barometric Pressure Release.

### How Robert I. Made the Right Decision and Got a Big Promotion

Robert I., a young executive I know, used this technique very successfully at a crucial moment in his business career.

An employee of a large corporation, he was suddenly offered a very substantial increase in salary by one of their competitors. When he told his boss of the offer, his boss made a counter-offer which did not seem quite as good as the other.

Robert I. had to decide on the spot. It was a tough day for making a decision. The air pressure was making him jumpy and nervous. Yet he had to say "yes" or "no." For some reason, a conversation I had had with him about Ultra-Barometrics flashed into his mind.

Without giving any outward sign, he slowed down his breathing and began to use the BPR technique to equalize his body pressure. In just a few minutes, his mind was calm enough to realize that his boss was testing him.

"I accept your offer, Mr. G., " he said, "I think this company has a lot more going for it than our competitor does."

His boss smiled. "I'm glad you said that, Bob. You see, we have you in mind for the post of Assistant Plant Manager. But we wanted to make sure that you're staying here because you believe in the company's future, and not just because of the money."

Bob never regretted that decision. Not only did he win his promised promotion, but about a year later, he heard that the other company was in serious financial trouble and had laid-off a quarter of their staff.

### Ultra-Calorics

There is one more invisible sign in the air that you must take into account, and that is the temperature. Due to such modern inventions as central heating and air conditioning, it is not as important as the others, since it is effective mainly out-of-doors.

However, occasionally it applies indoors as well. If you've ever been in an overheated or an overcooled building, you know how soon the temperature can start to bother you.

The important thing to know here is that different people do not react the same way to these temperature changes. As you will see when we get to the Psychonic Zodiac, some people are comfortable no matter how hot it gets, and others wilt if the temperature goes up 5 degrees. The same is true of cold.

Thus, before you can use the Ultra-Caloric temperature factor in your predictions, you need to know whether the person you're considering is sensitive to temperature changes, and if so, whether it is to heat or cold. This can be done by observation, of course, but there is an easier way. If you know the person's date of birth, you can sometimes make a prediction even if you've never met the person before.

Basically, the principle is that people born during the summer months are usually not bothered by heat, and people born during the winter months are not bothered by cold. Note that I said *usually*. If someone was born in a cold climate, they may not be able to take much heat, even if they were born in the summer. Or, if a baby was kept in an air-conditioned hospital until the following season, it may not react the way you would expect it to, if you went purely by its date of birth.

Thus, the only certain way of using Ultra-Calorics to predict and control the actions of others is through detailed observation and study, as well as watching the temperature closely.

### How Emma B. Had a Marvelous Trip to Europe

One of my relatives used the Ultra-Calorics technique to greatly improve her vacation last summer. Earlier in the year, when she was talking with her travel agent, she noticed that his mind seemed to be wandering, and that he hardly seemed to hear anything she said.

She gradually realized what was disturbing him—the room was almost freezing cold, due to an overefficient air conditioner. She immediately suggested that he turn the machine off, which he was only too happy to do. After a few cups of hot coffee, the travel agent was completely alert and on the ball.

He then set up one of the most marvelous vacations she had ever had, and even managed to get her a few discounts she hadn't expected. "All it took," she told me,"was to turn one tiny switch to the off position."

## THE AMAZING PSYCHONIC ZODIAC

As you saw in the section you just read on Ultra-Calorics, when and where you're born *does* make a difference in how you react to things.

Old-fashioned astrology, of course, carries this idea to extremes. Everyone is allotted one of 12 signs in an arrangement called a "zodiac," and this sign supposedly determines your fortune, love life and temperament. What's more, if someone misses being born under your sign by as little as a day or two, he has a completely different set of characteristics. Obviously, this simply does not work in real life situations.

Yet, like many ancient ideas, there is a germ of truth buried here. Hot-weather babies grow up with a different set of influences than cold-weather babies—during their most formative months, they're subjected to different influences: fresh air, pollen, dust, more oxygen, less clothing and so on.

Ultra-Astronics takes this truth, and incorporates it into the "Psychonic Zodiac." Examine the accompanying diagram carefully.

### How to Determine Whether Your Sign
### Is Krionox, Vernox, Estivox or Invernox

Generally speaking, you can determine your sign by comparing your date of birth with the dates shown for each sign in the accompanying Psychonic Zodiac diagram. But, unlike astrology, you are not ruled entirely by your date of birth. It is possible, for example, for someone to be born in the middle of July, and yet have a Krionox-type personality.

How can this be? A number of factors are at work. You might have been born in an air-conditioned hospital, for example, or in a cooler part of the world. Or your early personality might have been strongly influenced and controlled by Krionox parents. Examine the accompanying list, and decide which type of person you really are.

## THE PSYCHONIC ZODIAC

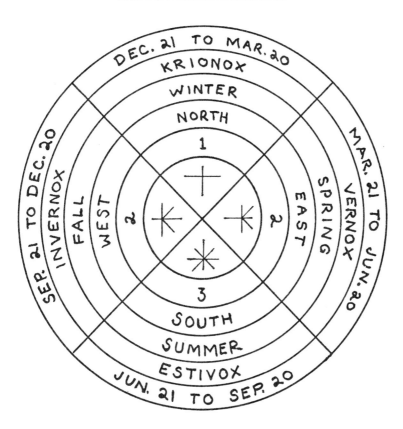

**KRIONOX (Dec. 21 to Mar. 20)**

*Symbol:* Leafless tree    *Psychonic Charge:* +1

The Krionox personality is very self-sufficient. You have a strong feeling of responsibility for your own destiny, and often achieve positions of great trust. Reliable, honest, able to carry out tough assignments, you are also sensitive and generous to your family and friends. Natural patience and a keen, quick perception make you very diplomatic when you want to be. Sometimes you become too critical of others, at other times too shy to say what you really mean. Frugality, a virtue, is occasionally carried to excess.

**VERNOX (Mar. 21 to Jun. 20)**

*Symbol:* Blooming tree          *Psychonic Charge:* +2

The Vernox personality is a doer, an energetic, proud and active person with great natural organizing and executive ability. You are good at earning all the money you need, but also good at spending it. You like large groups of people and are very outgoing and sociable, yet you have a deep, intense nature that most people never see. You sometimes act too abruptly, and later regret it. A deep devotion to those you care for sometimes turns to jealousy when others interfere. Too much curiosity sometimes creates problems.

### ESTIVOX (Jun. 21 to Sept. 20)

*Symbol:* Tree in full leaf          *Psychonic Charge:* +3

The Estivox personality is very emotional and creative in nature. Warm-hearted, affectionate, pleasant, you make friends easily. You are very determined and persevering, with excellent reasoning power and a sharp sense of proportion. You have a great love of home life and creature comforts, and are very loyal and industrious. You have a tendency to daydream, but often turn this to good advantage in the arts. Too much domestic comfort sometimes leads to becoming overweight, but this doesn't seem to bother you as much as it seems to bother others.

### INVERNOX (Sept. 21 to Dec. 20)

*Symbol:* Tree losing upper leaves  *Psychonic Charge:* +2

The Invernox personality is very neat, precise and reserved. Cautious, a careful dresser and very self-possessed, you tend to be an independent thinker. Your high intelligence gives you a deep understanding of human nature, and of the motives and reactions of others. You seldom speak your thoughts, but you have subtle, quiet ways of getting things done. Sometimes your reserve works against you and makes people hesitate to be friendly. Yet those who really know you value your friendship very highly. You are sometimes too intense.

* * * * *

"But," you say, "I don't precisely fit any of those definitions." You're right. Few people do, due to the factors we've already considered, such as a cool summer or a warm winter, and also for one other reason: the length of each cycle. Someone born, for example, at the end of winter, will find that he or she possesses some Vernox characteristics as well as the Krionox ones. You might say their Psychonic Charge is +1½.

This whole idea of four basic human types, incidentally, is far from new. The famous Greek doctor, Hippocrates, proposed a similar theory as early as 400 B.C., based on what he called "the four body fluids"—perhaps one of the earliest foreshadowings of the egonic flow theory.

## How Bernice F. Found Scores of Wonderful New Friends by P-Z Analysis

One useful application of the Psychonic Zodiac lies in the area of making new friends. Generally speaking, the closer someone is to your sign, the more likely it is that you two will be "simpatico."

An easy way to check this out is to subtract the Psychonic Charge of one sign from the other. For example, if you are a pure Estivox type (+3) and the other person is a pure Krionox (+1), your chances of hitting things off are somewhat less than if you were born closer in time to each other, assuming other things are equal. The principle here is that the closer the numerical value, the less the resistance to becoming friends.

Bernice F., a young teacher, used this principle to greatly improve her social life. New on the job, she found that many of the other teachers seemed to be unfriendly and hostile toward her. By discreet inquiries, she gradually discovered which teachers were born closest to her own sign. Then she made a point of seeking these teachers out and acting extra-friendly toward them. In a few short weeks, she suddenly found she had scores of wonderful new friends.

## How to Set Up Your Ultra-Astronic Chart

Is there a way you can predict your future actions, as well as the actions of others? Yes, by setting up an Ultra-Astronic Chart. Page 133 shows what one looks like.

To set up the chart, you fill it in as follows:

1. Put in subject's name (your own, if you are the subject).

2. Put in the prediction date—the day that you want to predict future actions on.

3. Put in the subject's sign. Look it up on the Psychonic Zodiac table if you are not sure what it is.

4. Subject's Psychonic Charge. See Psychonic Zodiac.

5. Seasonal Psychonic Charge. Again, see the Psychonic Zodiac to select the proper Psychonic Charge for the prediction date.

6. Subtract the smaller from the larger of the above two charges, and write the result in the proper column.

7. Add in the Ultra-Lunology factor. Look at a calendar to determine the nearest quarter of the moon for the prediction date, and use the number shown on the Chart under Moon Phase.

8. Add in the Ultra-Ionic and Ultra-Barometric factors. Since their effect is usually somewhat milder, they are combined into one unit under Ionic/Barometric Charge. Check the weather forecast for the prediction date, and place the proper number in the column shown.

9. Now add up all the numbers in the second column. The total represents the total Ultra-Astronic Charge operating on the subject on the prediction date.

## How to Read Your Ultra-Astronic Chart

The total Ultra-Astronic Charge is a highly significant figure. It tells you exactly what your own or your subject's emotional state of mind is on a given date. Here is how to interpret it:

*Charge = 2:* Conditions are ideal for getting what you want from the subject. Subject is calm, relaxed and in a friendly mood. Now is the time to ask for a raise, a date, a favor or anything else you desire.

*Charge = 4:* Subject is slightly agitated, but is still fairly calm. You can still get what you want, but it should be approached much more carefully and slowly. A strong sales pitch should be used.

*Charge = 6:* The subject is starting to get very "up-tight," and is nervous and irritable. Little chance of getting what you want now—your best bet is to wait a while. Concentrate on being friendly and helpful.

```
ULTRA-ASTRONIC CHART

        Subject's  Name____Bernice F._____

        Prediction Date____Dec. 22, 1974_____

        Subject's Sign ____Krionox_____
```

| | | |
|---|---|---|
| A.. Subject's Psychonic Charge | +1 | |
| B . Seasonal Psychonic Charge | +1 | |
| C . Difference between A. & B. | | O |
| D . Moon Phase: Prediction Date  1● 2◑ 3○ 2◐  Select # next to nearest ¼ | | I |
| E. Ionic/Barometric Charge  1:Calm    2:Pre-storm  3:Storm    2:Post-storm | | 3 |
| F. TOTAL ULTRA-ASTRONIC CHARGE | | 4 |

*Charge = 8:* Subject is in an extremely tense and aggravated state. Do not cross his or her path if you can help it. Be as agreeable as possible, and do not try to solicit any favors—it's virtually impossible now.

The lowest possible Ultra-Astronic Charge is 2, and the maximum is 8. Charges of 3, 5 and 7 produce emotional states in-between the ones described, and can easily be estimated.

## How to Get a Reading When You Have Only Partial Data

Perhaps you're wondering how you can set up an Ultra-Astronic Chart when you don't have all the data you need. If, for example, you were trying to set up a chart for a stranger, you might not know his birthday. Or you might be setting up a chart so far ahead that you don't have a clear weather prediction for the date involved.

One problem you *won't* have is selecting the Moon Phase number, since you can look this up on a calendar or in an almanac for at least a year ahead.

But, let us suppose you don't know someone's birthday. In such a case, you would select an average value for the subject's psychonic charge—a standard +2. The seasonal psychonic charge would stay the same, since it depends only on the prediction date.

The Ionic/Barometric charge number is also easily adjusted. If you do not have a firm weather report for the date involved, use a standard value of +2.

Naturally, an Ultra-Astronic Chart set up this way is not going to be as precise or as helpful as one where you have all the data entered exactly, but it can still be useful.

For example, if you were going to meet someone whose birthday you didn't know, but you did know that the moon would be in its first phase (new), and that the weather would be calm, your Ultra-Astronic Chart for June 21st might read like this:

| | | |
|---|---|---|
| Subject's Psychonic Charge | +2 | |
| (estimated) | | |
| Seasonal Psychonic Charge | +3 | |
| Difference .......................... | | 1 |
| Moon Phase .......................... | | 1 |
| Ionic/Barometric Charge ................. | | 1 |
| TOTAL ULTRA-ASTRONIC CHARGE ..... | | 3 |

This would indicate that conditions are almost ideal for getting your way with the person in question. Even if he turned out to be a Krionox, with a psychonic charge of +1, this would only increase the total charge to 4, which is still a favorable situation.

### How to Get a Quick On-the-Spot Reading in Less than Five Minutes

As you have seen, Ultra-Astronic chart construction is very rapid, compared to the involved procedures of old-fashioned astrology. However, if you want to speed things up even more, here is how to do it:

1. Keep a pocket calendar in your wallet or purse with the phases of the moon marked on it. A solid circle can be used to mark the new moon, a hollow circle can be used to mark the full moon and the other phases can be marked simply with an "X" through the date.

2. Make up some Ultra-Astronic Chart forms on 3x5 file cards and keep a few in your pocket or purse.

3. Five minutes before you meet someone, fill in as much data as you can on the form. You will know the season, the moon phase and the weather conditions, so the only thing remaining is the subject's psychonic charge. This can either be estimated, as you saw earlier, or filled in completely if you know the subject's date of birth. A good way to discover a person's birthday is to see if they are wearing any astrological jewelry. Here's a quick conversion table:

> KRIONOX covers Capricorn, Aquarius, Pisces
> VERNOX covers Aries, Taurus, Gemini
> ESTIVOX covers Cancer, Leo, Virgo
> INVERNOX covers Libra, Scorpio, Sagittarius

It fits fairly closely, although the dates at the beginning and end of each Psychonic Zodiac sign are a few days off.

## WHAT ULTRA-ASTRONICS CAN DO FOR YOU

In this chapter, you have seen how to read the messages in the sky that really can help you. You've discovered:

- How the moon rules the minds of men and women, and how you can use the techniques of Ultra-Lunology to predict their actions.

- How a slight change in the electrical "smell" of the air can make others calm or nervous, and how you can control this effect on yourself with the Egonic Palming technique.

- How barometric highs and lows also influence people's emotions, and how you can use BPR breathing to reduce this influence on yourself.

- How the Ultra-Caloric factor can sometimes play an important part in determining how people act, and how you can use this knowledge to your advantage.

- How to determine your Ultra-Astronic sign in the Psychonic Zodiac, and set up a useful chart you can use to predict and control the actions of others.

But above all, the techniques of Ultra-Astronics give you powerful information about yourself:

- You see when you are likely to be most irritable and when you will be most calm—an important bit of knowledge when you find yourself in a situation where you have to make an important decision or "sell" your ideas to someone. A high reading on the Ultra-Astronic Chart warns you to go slow, while the Egonic Palming and BPR breathing techniques let you overcome the forces acting on you, at least partially, and enable you to do the right thing.

- You discover which periods of the year and of each month are the most dangerous for you, and can thus make arrangements to protect your interests. For example, if you know that a particular day has the potential of a +8 psychonic charge for you, you can avoid doing certain actions, such as asking your boss for a raise or cooking an elaborate meal.

- You find out when your artistic, creative and psychic powers are at their peak—when your psychonic charge is at its absolute minimum—and can use this information to dramatically increase the quantity and quality of your work.

- Finally, you have the satisfaction of knowing that your prediction and control methods really work, while all around you, you see people trying to use slipshod, old-fashioned astrology, and making a mess of things. Best of all, once you know *their* astrological sign, you can use it to understand them, while their knowing yours will tell them absolutely nothing.

# 8

## *ULTRA-DIVINATION:*
## *How*
## *to Find*
## *Hidden Treasures*

---

Why is it that some people seem to have a mysterious ability to find things? Why can others find precious minerals, oil, water and hidden treasures on land and under the sea?

These are far from idle questions. All over the world, research is now being conducted to find out the secret that lies behind this amazing ability.

The Russians, for example, are now spending over 12 million rubles a year on psychic research—and a good part of this money is being devoted to water divining and dowsing for all kinds of things.

"There is nothing mystical in the ability of the human body to react to underground mines or water." That statement comes, not from some wild-eyed prophet, but from Dr. A. Ogilvy, Chairman of the Geology Department of Moscow State University.

The phenomenon is called "radiesthesia" (sensitivity to radiation), and it is one of the oldest psychic powers known to man. How old? The Great Emperor Yu of

Ancient China appears in a painting done around 2200 B.C. carrying a dowsing rod. The ancient Egyptians, too, appear in carvings of water finders carrying these rods.

And in the Bible itself, there are references to rods that were used to discover water. In Chapter 17 of *Exodus,* for example, it is related how Moses took a *rod* and brought water forth in the midst of the wilderness. Was this a dowsing rod? The Bible does not say.

Down through the ages, the dowsing rod has been used all over the world, despite the objections of so-called "wise men" who could not understand it. Even in the recent Viet Nam War, U.S. Army Engineers experimented with dowsing rods to locate underground tunnels, unexploded shells and nonmetallic mines and booby traps—and found that the dowsing rods really helped!

## How Ultra-Divination Works

Now, this chapter is not going to tell you how to make these ordinary types of dowsing rods. That type of information is easily available, and it is not what this book is about.

There are Ultra-Psychonic devices that make an ordinary dowsing rod seem like a candle compared to a bonfire. You're going to find out about them very shortly. But first, here's the kind of results they can produce for you:

• You will discover how to charge your body with Ultra-Divination power, so that in effect your entire being becomes a Geocosmic Dowsing Rod with unlimited potential!

• You will find out how to build a Psychonic Radar Locator for just a few pennies that can guide you unerringly to buried wealth!

• You will see how this same device can be modified to find underwater treasure!

• You will peer into the Hidden Universe and discover the astonishing secret of the Anti-Particles and their mighty powers!

• You will discover the unusual ways you can use Ultra-Divination to bring back a lost love and repair a disintegrating romance!

• You will behold the amazing "Miracle Map" that finds lost relatives and draws them back to you like a magnet!

• You will learn the wonder-working "Recovery Chant" that makes lost or stolen objects return seemingly of their own accord!

"Is all this possible?" you ask. It certainly is, and you're about to discover how such incredible claims can be made.

## The Amazing Anti-Particles from the Hidden Universe

But before we proceed to the actual methods and techniques involved, a word of explanation is necessary.

You may recall that in Chapter 1, we looked inside the Psychic Atom, and discovered that it was composed of Psychons, Ultrons and Egons. And, at that time, I mentioned the possibility of an Anti-Universe.

Well, some scientists today say that such a Universe really exists. It is a very strange place: The speed of light, for example, is the *slowest* anything can move. Time runs backwards. Things that are solid in our universe are transparent in the other, and vice versa. Gravity repels instead of attracting. And so on.

The proof that the Anti-Universe is actually there has been developing slowly for several decades. In 1929, Dr. P. A. Dirac conceived the idea that "empty space" is actually tightly packed with electrons of *negative mass*. They are called anti-electrons, and within a few years, these particles were actually photographed.

Then, in 1955, four West Coast physicists announced the discovery and observation of anti-protons. Finally, in the fall of 1956, the giant Bevatron at the University of California enabled scientists to detect anti-neutrons.

What does this mean? It means that anti-matter really exists, and that *there must be an Anti-Universe to contain it!*

It is my belief that—just as our own Universe contains mental particles like Psychons, Ultrons and Egons—so, too, the Anti-Universe contains Anti-Psychons, Anti-Ultrons and Anti-Egons.

If these Anti-Particles exist—and I am convinced they do—many previously "impossible" psychic feats have a perfectly simple and rational explanation.

Time-travel, clairvoyance, the ability to appear in two places at once and even more incredible powers can now be understood as manifestations of the surging energies of the Anti-Particles.

Thus, the long-known "psychic mystery" of dowsing has at last been solved, for example. Just as the psychonic and ultronic beams are able to penetrate the nooks and crannies of other people's minds, the anti-psychonic and anti-ultronic beams are able to penetrate solid matter—actually let you look through walls, see buried riches under the earth or under water and even locate people whom you have "lost" somewhere along the time track.

## How to Generate the Anti-Laser Beams

Generating the anti-psychonic and anti-ultronic laser beams becomes a simple matter once you understand this basic theory.

Here, for example, is the procedure for turning on the Anti-Psychon Generator in your brain and placing it under conscious control:

1. Lie down in a dark, quiet room. Close your eyes and concentrate on a field of golden light, imagining the entire Anti-Universe to be filled with its radiant energy.

2. Now, imagine a tiny point of deep, solid black, right in the center of your head.

3. Concentrate on the black point for five minutes every day, until it appears instantly whenever you will it into being.

This black point is actually the forefront of a beam of Anti-Psychons emerging into our Universe. Here is how to focus this beam:

1. Turn on your Anti-Psychon Generator, in a lighted room.

2. Imagine that a stream of solid black rays is emerging from your eyes, and that your eyes are concentrating this stream, just as a magnifying glass concentrates the rays of the sun.

3. Focus on an object 6 inches away from your eyes, and imagine that the two black streams are both concentrated on it.

4. Now move the focus of the black streams *inside* the object you are concentrating on. Gradually, it will become transparent to your gaze, and you will (with practice) become able to "feel" its texture and structure.

5. After you have mastered this, start to gradually increase the range of your focus to a foot, then to 2 feet and so on. When you reach a distance of about 4 feet, start to see if you can penetrate the walls and floors of the building you are in.

6. Continue to develop this ability out-of-doors, until you can "see" deep into the earth at will. You have now mastered the Anti-Psychonic Laser.

In a later chapter, you will discover how to generate the Anti-Ultronic Laser, and use it to "see" through time. It is of limited utility in Ultra-Divination, however, so we will pass over it for the moment.

## The Secret of Anti-Egonic Flow

Anti-Egons, on the other hand, are vitally involved in certain types of Ultra-Divination. Just as egon particles are charged with Growth Force and are intimately concerned with life, health and memory—anti-egons are charged with Accumulation Force and are concerned with absence of life, sickness and forgetfulness.

Here is how to stimulate your anti-egonic flow:

1. Lie in a darkened room, and generate an egonic flow, as explained in Chapter 1, running down both arms and back to your brain. Get the "feel" of it, and fix the sensation firmly in your mind.

2. Now, try to sense the other parts of your body that are *not* involved in the egonic flow, such as your legs. At first, you will have difficulty in noticing anything. Gradually, you will become aware of a sort of "counter flow." It may manifest itself at first as a feeling of weakness, or of irritation, or even as an itch.

3. Eventually, you will be able to feel the complete circuit it makes between the parts of your body not experiencing egonic flow and your brain. Do not continue the experience too long— you may find it a bit unpleasant, for one thing—and it is only necessary for you to become aware of it, not to intensify it.

## How to Charge Yourself with Ultra-Divination Power

As you have probably guessed by now, Ultra-Divination is based mainly on variations of the Anti-Psychonic forces, supplemented by the Anti-Egonic flow.

Before any of the devices described in this chapter will work for you, however, it is necessary for you to charge yourself with Ultra-Divination Power. Here's how you do it:

1. Close your eyes and concentrate on the field of golden light that comprises the Anti-Universe.

2. In the center of the golden field, picture exactly what you are going to look for, whether it be buried treasure, gold or whatever.

3. Now, from the center of the object, let the black Anti-Psychon beam emerge, and bring it to a focus in the area you intend to search. For example, if you are looking for gold, imagine a box

of gold coins in the center of the field, with black rays shooting from it out through your eyes and into the ground. As you walk along through the search area, you will feel a "tingling" sensation as you approach any gold coins that are buried there.

4. As you get closer and closer to your goal, gradually "blank out" your other bodily sensations by lightly increasing your awareness of your body's anti-egonic flow. In effect, try to forget you even have a body, and concentrate on the "tingling" sensation.

Your body is now charged to the maximum with Ultra-Divination power!

## How Ward M. Found a Lost Will

A friend of mine, Ward M., recently found a long-lost will by means of this technique. A collector of antiques, he recently purchased an old desk from the 19th Century for his den. To his surprise, he began to feel "vibrations" from it as soon as it was delivered. Sensitizing his Ultra-Divination power, he seemed to be able to "see through" a part of the desk that looked perfectly solid. A closer examination followed, and he noticed a hairline crack that was almost invisible. He tried moving the area in various ways, and suddenly a little drawer slid out. In it was an old document from the 1860's—a will made out by a soldier about to leave for the battlefront. Although the property bequeathed by the will was of a minor nature, Ward was able to sell the will itself to an antique dealer for over $100.

## Building a Psychonic Radar Locator
## for Less than $1.00

As I said earlier, dowsing rods are all right as far as they go, but there's a much better tool to use. It's called a "Psychonic Radar Locator," and you can build one for less than $1.00.

It consists simply of a piece of nylon cord with a weight on the end of it—a pendulum. Of course, there are certain requirements.

For one thing, the nylon cord must be *unused*. The best way to get such a cord is to purchase a roll of fishing tackle at your local sporting goods store. A 50-foot roll will cost much less than $1.00 and will give you enough cord for scores of treasure hunts.

The weight should consist of a sample of what you're looking for. If you're looking for gold, for example, you should suspend a gold object from the cord. It does not have to be exactly the same as what you're looking for—a gold ring will do, even if you're looking for coins, for instance—but the closer it comes to the exact object you're looking for, the better your chances of success.

To use your Psychonic Radar Locator, cut off exactly 1 foot of cord and attach the proper pendulum weight. Then, after charging your body with Ultra-Divination power as previously explained, stand in the center of the search area and hold the end of the pendulum in your right hand. (If you are normally left-handed, hold it in your left hand.)

The pendulum will gradually start to swing back and forth. Note the direction it is swinging in and walk along that line. When you get directly over the object you're looking for, the pendulum will start to swing in a circle.

That's all there is to it, except to note that occasionally the pendulum will swing in a circle right at the start. This usually indicates that either the object you're searching for is not in the search area or someone else is deliberately interfering with your search. In such a case, your best bet is to stop and try again at a future time.

To increase your sensitivity, try this Ultra-Divination Tuning Ritual:

1. Collect several cardboard boxes with covers.

2. Ask a friend to place an object in one of them while you are out of the room.

3. Make a Psychonic Radar Locator, charge your body with Ultra-Divination power and try to spot the box that the object is hidden in.

The more you perform this ritual, the more sensitive you will become to this type of activity, and the greater success you will have when you attempt it in the field.

Naturally, if you plan to search for a particular type of wealth, such as gold or oil, for example, you should use this type of object in the ritual, so that your body will become especially "tuned" to it.

**How Evelyn P. Found 12 Oil Wells**

Do some people have "natural" control of their Ultra-Divination powers? An astonishing report from Australia would seem to indicate so.

Evelyn P., who used the pendulum technique over a map to locate gold and silver mines, refined her map-dowsing technique one step further: she simply ran her fingers over a map with her eyes shut, while an associate wrote down what she said. Silver and radium ores seemed to produce a burning sensation in her fingers, while oil made her feel as though she were in a dirty fog, and gold and diamonds produced a feeling of frustration.

The ultimate test of her powers came in 1952, when she was sent a map of a certain area of the U.S. by an American, and asked to mark it for oil. She returned the map with 2,000 acres marked in red. Since that date, 12 producing oil wells have been found in the area she marked out, while wells drilled outside of her marks came in dry.

### Finding Things Underwater Using "Map Dowsing"

The method she used, incidentally, "map-dowsing"—is the only practical way to prospect for things underwater. Direct locating is virtually impossible, since the pendulum would be moved constantly by the motion of the water, whether you're sitting in a boat or swimming beneath the surface.

Since few people possess Evelyn P.'s natural dowsing talent, the Psychonic Radar Locator technique is practically a necessity. Another requirement is a fairly large, good clear map of the water area you want to cover. Nautical charts, showing the depth of the water in each section of the map, are perhaps the best to use, since they can guide you to the most easily recoverable wealth.

The map should be placed on a table, and you should stand over it, holding the pendulum, with your eyes closed to reduce distracting influences. A friend should work with you, so that you can call out the areas to be marked.

### How Malcolm C. Located a Fortune in Pirate Gold

There is a tiny island in the Pacific with not just one, but *three* treasure troves buried on it by pirates! Called Cocos Island, this little scrap of land has tons of silver ingots, chests stuffed with jewels and pieces-of-eight, and over $100 million dollars in Inca gold hidden on it somewhere.

Some years back, an explorer named Malcolm C. decided to use psychic channels to see if the treasure could be found. He contacted a certain Miss J. and gave her a map of the island, with its name hidden. When she tried her divining rod over the map, it went into oscillation over certain spots entirely different from those Malcolm C. had thought were the likely ones.

Before Malcolm C. could capitalize on this knowledge, the Depression wiped out most of his funds, and he was never able to cash in on the information Miss J. had given him. Today, the entire treasure is still waiting to be found on that tiny bit of land halfway between San Francisco and Valparaiso.

### How to Bring Back True Love

Ultra-Divination has many other uses besides finding treasure, of course. One of the most popular is to find a missing lover and make that person return to you.

Here's how it works: The missing lover's photo is pasted onto a piece of heavy cardboard in the shape of triangle, thusly:

The entire triangle is suspended by the usual piece of nylon cord, and after you have charged yourself with Ultra-Divination power, you simply move it over a map of the city or area where you think your missing love may be. When you get directly over the place where your lover is now living, the point of the triangle will start to move in a circle. As the point moves, say this Summoning Chant:

(Lover,) return to me.
Wherever you may be,
In the outside world so wide,
Come back swiftly to my side.

As you say the chant, try to project along with it a strong feeling of sexiness and love. Use the person's real name instead of "lover."

### How Dinah B. Brought Back Her Runaway Husband and Made Him Be True

A woman I know recently used a variation of this technique

with great effectiveness. Dinah B., a nurse, was left in the lurch about a year ago when her husband ran off with another woman.

Dinah used the above technique every morning when she woke up, and every night just before she went to sleep. In between times, being a religious woman, she put the photo of her husband (triangle and all) in her Bible, in the middle of the Song of Solomon.

Within a week, she heard that her husband had broken up with the other woman, and a few days later, he appeared outside her door, begging to be forgiven. "He is a changed man," she told me, "and I don't think he'll ever do that again."

## The Astounding "Miracle Map"
## That Finds Lost Relatives

Now, in the sections you've just read, you've seen how people have been able to locate things using a "dowsing map." The maps they used were ordinary ones, but they were charged with the Ultra-Divination power that radiated from the people who used them.

Finding lost relatives is somewhat more difficult than finding either buried treasure or missing lovers. For one thing, the distance involved is usually greater. Also, the emotional charge is somewhat less intense in some cases, and the desire to return is usually weaker.

Thus, something must be strengthened in the finding process, and since the pendulum is already at its maximum charge, only the map is left. Luckily, there is an Ultra-Psychonic technique that has exactly the desired effect.

You may recall that, in Chapter 3, you discovered how to "impregnate" a letter with an ultronic beam. The same technique can be used with a map, if it is the folding kind. All that needs to be done is to fold the map all the way up, and place it on your forehead for about 30 seconds while you project the beam of ultrons through it. You now have what is called a "Miracle Map."

Such a Miracle Map should be prepared as closely as possible to the actual dowsing session, of course, as the ultronic charge will gradually weaken with the passage of time.

## How Ethel D. Found Her Long-Lost Son
## and Brought Him Home

Ethel D. used the Miracle Map method, together with the

Photo Triangle variation of the Psychonic Radar Locator to discover the whereabouts of her teen-age son, who had been missing for several years. To her dismay, when she checked with the local authorities in that area, she discovered that her son was living in a hippie commune, and had become involved with drugs.

Using a technique similar to that used by Dinah B., she put her son's Photo Triangle in her family Bible every night in the *Book of Exodus,* and prayed that he would be delivered from the slavery he was in.

Exactly one month later, to the day, after she had started this, her phone rang. It was her son. To her delight, he wanted to come home "for a visit." Once home, she managed to convince him he needed professional help, and he is now enrolled in a Methadone program, and has the first steady job he has ever held.

## An Unusual Ultra-Divination Technique
## for Finding Lost Pets

Another variation of the above technique can be used to find lost pets. Since, in many cases, a photo of the pet is not available, a drawing or photo of a similar animal should be cut out of a magazine, and mounted on the triangle. The animal's name should be written on a slip of paper, and pasted onto the center of the picture.

The Summoning Chant should be used, as previously explained, and said once every morning and once every evening. Between times, the Photo Triangle should be placed in your Bible in Chapter 8 of the *Book of Genesis,* which describes how the animals were summoned into the Ark.

## How Sam and Irma Found Their Missing Cat

This technique was used with great effectiveness recently by two of my neighbors, whose cat had been missing for several days. After trying the technique for exactly one day, their cat turned up the following morning, looking a little bit worse for wear, but in fairly good shape nevertheless.

Some other people I know were able to locate their dog in a dog pound many miles away from their home, and arrived to claim him just in time. "Your technique saved his life," they told me.

## The Anti-Psychonic "Recovery Chant" That
## Summons Back Lost or Stolen Objects

Sometimes inanimate objects seem to take on a life of their own. If you've ever dropped a nail or a key, or a coin—and have been unable to find it, no matter how hard you've looked—you know just what I mean.

It's even worse when the missing object is part of a set, like a sock or an earring or a piece of silverware.

Naturally, the preceding techniques can be used, but they take a bit of adaption. Few of us have a map of household areas, and if the loss happens away from home, your chances of using the triangle or even the pendulum methods are pretty slim.

Here's what to do when you can't use them:

1. Hold a similar object in your closed fist. If it is part of a set, hold another piece of the set.

2. Close your eyes, and visualize the golden field of the Anti-Universe, with the missing object in the center of it.

3. Hum this Anti-Psychonic "Recovery Chant" slowly:

> "Come, come, come to me,
> Come to (name) do!
> Come, come, come to me,
> And I'll come to you!

This need not be hummed aloud, but can be done as silently as you like, depending on where you are at the time. Your first name should be substituted for (name) where it appears in the Chant.

4. As you continue to do this, the golden field of the Anti-Universe will gradually fade away, and you will see the actual surroundings of the missing object. They may be a little hard to recognize at first, but you will gradually be able to match them up to the search area. Go to the place indicated, and you will find the lost object.

If the object has been stolen from you, this technique will not guide you to it, since you will not recognize its location. However, the "Recovery Chant" has unusual magnetic powers in such cases, and powerful forces will begin to work on it to draw it back to you.

## How Marion T. Got Back Her Missing Jewelry

An example of this is the case of Marion T., who I met in Europe some years ago. She was extremely upset over the theft of a diamond ring that had been in her family for many years. I introduced her to the "Recovery Chant," and within 48 hours, the ring turned up.

She received a call from the local police office and was asked to come there to identify her jewelry. Sure enough, there was the ring. "Where did it come from?" she asked the police officer.

"It's very strange," he replied. "We found it in the pocket of a man who had fallen into the Arno River and drowned. He died about 48 hours ago."

### How to Make Money Finding Things for Others

An easy and pleasant way to supplement your income is to practice these techniques until you become an expert at them. You'll then find you have an extremely marketable talent.

Start helping your friends and co-workers to find things, and before long people will start to come to you and ask you to find things for them for money. A fair fee is 10% of the object's value.

## WHAT ULTRA-DIVINATION CAN DO FOR YOU

In this chapter, you've seen:

- How a mighty Invisible World co-exists with our own, and how you can reach into it for power.
- How to generate an Anti-Psychonic Laser Beam that will let you see through walls and other solid objects by willpower alone.
- How to fill your entire being with the surging energy called Ultra-Divination Power, and discover the secret of limitless wealth.
- How to put together a Psychonic Radar Locator for a few pennies that will guide you to lost riches, missing relatives and much more.
- How to use the mysterious Anti-Psychonic "Recovery Chant" that turns up lost or stolen articles as if by magic.
- How to perform "map dowsing" and use the astonishing "Miracle Map" to find things without leaving your home.

... It almost sounds too good to be true. But I think you'll be more than delighted when you put Ultra-Divination to work for you and watch the hidden treasures appear.

# 9

## ULTRA-MAGIC:

### How to
### Invoke the Secret
### Forces of Nature

Does magic really work? Today, after years of skepticism, more and more people are starting to believe that it does.

Charlie W. is one of them. After six years of marriage, he found himself on the verge of bankruptcy. No matter how hard or how long he worked, he just couldn't seem to make enough money to feed his wife and four kids. So when a friend suggested that he use one of the new Ultra-Magic spells to solve his problems, he was willing to give it a try. He followed the instructions.

Suddenly, things began to break wide open for him. To his amazement, a letter came in the mail advising him that a relative he hadn't seen for years had died and left him $20,000. Then an insurance company paid off on a claim he had just about given up on. Finally, he won $50,000 in the state lottery.

Disbelievers don't bother Charlie. He laughs all the way to the bank. At long last, Ultra-Psychonics is working *for* him, instead of against him.

### The Astonishing Power of Ultra-Magic

Money started rolling in for Charlie once he began to use the Ultra-Magic technique called "money polarization." It's a "spell"—not the old-fashioned kind with bats and toads—but a new discovery, a technique that's as modern and up-to-date as a color TV set.

Here's what this new Ultra-Magic technique can do for you:

- You can start to have dozens of new friends of both sexes, all eager to please you and do whatever you want.
- You can make "good luck" your normal way of life—start it flowing to you endlessly and automatically.
- You can make your loved ones more affectionate and responsive, willing to grant your every desire without hesitation.
- You can defend yourself against people who are using black magic and witchcraft against you, and strike back with devastating force and power.
- You can discover the hidden meaning of signs and omens that most people overlook, so that the locked book of the future will fall open to your sight.
- You can make powerful amulets and talismans that will protect you against the powers of darkness.
- You can invoke invisible, benevolent beings to help you succeed in whatever you undertake.

Ultra-Magic is an entirely new science, yet it is based on principles thousands of years old. For the first time in recorded history, the arcane wisdom of the ages has been sorted out, scientifically examined, de-fantasized and re-integrated into a proven system that, under the correct conditions, works every time without fail.

Unlike ordinary magic, there is no "white" or "black" Ultra-Magic. Its principles and techniques can be learned, mastered and used by any man or woman willing to make the effort, and it is entirely compatible with the teachings of all the world's major religions.

### The Mighty Power Behind Ultra-Magic

Open practically any book of old-fashioned "magic" and you

will make a startling discovery: the metal *iron* must never be used.‾
In case after case you will read how magical gold was turned to
dust and ashes when touched with iron, how spells were broken
with steel swords and many similar instances.

The reasons for this go back more than 10,000 years, to the
Age of Bronze, when principles of magic were first discovered.
Iron was unknown, and when it appeared on the scene, there was
no place for it in the spells, rituals and incantations of the time.
Furthermore, its introduction into a situation "broke" the magical
requirements, due to iron's amazing psychonic powers.

So, for centuries, iron was not used in magic.

Yet, when the scientific methods of Ultra-Psychonics were
applied to magic a few years ago, an astounding fact was revealed:
not only could iron be used in spells, but if it was used properly, it
was the most powerful magical ingredient of all!

The reason for this is simple: iron is the only metal that can
react to the Earth's titanic magnetic field. This principle is used in
a thousand different ways today: in compass needles, in the giant
electric generators that light our cities, even in atomic bombs and
space rockets. Yet until now, no one has ever applied the magnetic
powers of iron to magic, using the principles of Ultra-Psychonics.

That is what Ultra-Magic is: the new science of Magical
Phenomena, based on the properties of iron. And it's like a miracle
come true!

## ULTRA-MAGIC SPELLS THAT CAN HELP YOU

### The Magnetic Spell That Brings Friendship

Buy a flat piece of wood, exactly 3½ inches wide, 1½ inches
thick and 12 inches long. You can get this at any lumberyard by
asking for a 1-foot piece of 2x4 lumber. The cost should be under
50¢.

With a pencil, print your name on one side of the wood, in
letters 1 inch high. Now turn the wood over and print the name
of the person you want to be more friendly with on the other side.
Both names should be centered on the wood. A good way to do
this is to write the names on a piece of paper the same size as the
wood, and then trace off the letters so that they are evenly
centered.

Next, take an all-steel hammer and drive ordinary flat-headed
nails, 1 inch long, into the letters of each name. You will probably

feel some of the nails touch. It is helpful if they do so, but not vital. Overlap the nail heads in each letter, so that they are all connected.

Next, take an ordinary table lamp and attach a long extension cord to it. Do not plug it in. Wrap one turn of the extension cord around the piece of wood for every letter in your name. Then plug in the cord and turn on the lamp. As you turn on the lamp, say the following:

> Iron magnets set in rows
> Power comes and power goes
> Name to name the current flows
> Power comes and power goes
> Make this name my friend.

Turn off the lamp. Repeat this once every evening exactly at sunset for seven days. Every morning following the spell, you must seek out the person you are trying to make your friend, and greet him or her by name. Then you must talk to him or her for at least 60 seconds. The subject of the conversation is not important—it can be about the weather, his or her health, sports, hobbies or anything else that is not controversial—just so a psychonic flow is started.

After one week, discontinue the spell. Pull all the nails out of the board and burn it. The nails should be put in a cloth bag and thrown into running water. Continue the morning greeting and talk for three weeks more. The person involved will be your friend from then on.

## The Magnetic Spell That Attracts Good Luck

Place ten new $1 bills in a green bowl. Close your eyes, and select one bill out of the 10. Then wrap the bill around a small horseshoe-shaped magnet, and wrap nine pieces of wax paper, 6 inches square, around the bill and magnet. Fold each piece down as small as possible around the preceding one.

Place 1 inch of peat moss in a flower pot painted green. Put the wax paper package containing the magnet and $1 bill on top of the peat moss. Now add more peat moss until the flower pot is almost full. Sprinkle mung beans on the surface of the peat moss, and cover them over with about 1/2 inch more peat moss. Then pour water on top and say the following magnetic spell:

> The soil is wet at my command
> Magnet, magnet in the land
> Give my luck a helping hand

> Grow, beans, grow
> Grow, money, grow

Water the pot every day until the beans start to sprout. Dig up the sprouts and eat them at sunset. No other food should be eaten that evening. The next day, only green-colored foods and water may be eaten until sunset. At sunset, dig up the package with the magnet and the dollar bill. The magnet should be kept in a jar full of pennies, and lottery tickets should be placed under it. The dollar bill must be given to the first charity that asks for help, either in person or by mail, after you take it out of the pot. Burn the wax paper.

Once this is done, a radical change will take place in your luck, and things will start to go the way you want.

### The Magnetic Love Spell That Never Fails

For the man who wants to attract a certain woman, the procedure is as follows:

Put an unused roll of recording tape into a tape recorder. Record the following:

> Magnet draw my love to me
> Make her be what she must be
> Bring her to me, make her true
> Make her do what she must do

Cut off the piece of recorded tape and wrap it around your left wrist several times. Fasten the end with a piece of Scotch tape. Wear the tape for 12 days and nights, and the woman you want will be irresistibly drawn to you. Be careful not to get the tape wet, however, as this will cancel the spell.

For the woman who wants to attract a certain man, the spell is similar. Put an unused roll of tape into a tape recorder. Record the following:

> Magnet draw my love to me
> Make him be what he must be
> Bring him to me, make him true
> Make him do what he must do

Cut off the piece of tape and split it into two equal halves. Wrap each half around one of your ankles, and tape the end down with Scotch tape. Wear the tape every night for 12 nights. Take it off every morning. Be careful not to get the tape wet or the spell will be cancelled.

## Spell Brings Man to Her from 200 Miles Away

An interesting example of the power of this spell was recently reported to me by a former schoolteacher now living in the vicinity of New York City. Recently, her boyfriend broke up with her and moved to Boston. She immediately began using the magnetic spell, and on the morning of the twelfth night her phone rang. It was her boyfriend. "I just couldn't stand it in Boston," he told her. "It was as if there was something pulling at me all the time to come back to you."

A month later they were married.

## How to Defend Yourself Against Black Magic and Witchcraft

Are things going well for you? Or do you find that nothing seems to work out the way you want it to. You can't seem to get ahead at work. You have strange pains in parts of your body that never hurt you before. Old friends seem to be avoiding you.

Perhaps you may be the victim of a black magic spell, from a known or unknown enemy. Luckily, Ultra-Magic offers several excellent defenses and exorcisms against such attacks by witchcraft, since it is more powerful than anything the old magic is capable of generating, and is solidly based on the laws of Ultra-Psychonics.

## Counter-Attacking a Known Enemy

This Ultra-Magic spell is based on one that goes back 4,000 years to ancient Egypt, but modernized so as to increase its effectiveness a hundredfold. The only requirement is that you know who your secret enemy is. Make sure you are right, as this spell can do a lot of damage to an innocent person as well as to a guilty one.

The first step is to buy a beef heart at your local butcher shop. Next you must "baptize" it. This is done by writing the person's name in red ink on a piece of paper cut into the shape of a heart. The paper should be burned in a clean dish, and the ashes rubbed all over the real heart, as you say:

> This is the double, the heart of my enemy
> As God is my witness, I name it (name of person)

The next step is to stick steel pins into the heart, one pin for each letter of your enemy's name, saying the letter out loud as you push in the pin. When this is complete, touch the heads of the pins with a small magnet. Then wrap the heart in aluminum foil and put it into your oven. As you turn on the oven, say:

> It is not this heart that I mean to burn
> But (the person's) heart that I wish to turn
> Wishing (him/her) neither peace nor rest
> Till (he/she) is dead and gone

Keep the heart in the oven for several hours, until it starts to burn and smoke. Take it out of the oven, and plunge it into cold water. The next morning, the heart should be thrown out in the garbage.

### How Rudy Cured His Stomach Pains

Does this spell work? Ask Rudy B. of Detroit. After having a violent argument with a neighbor who lived across the street, he was stricken with terrible pains in his stomach that just wouldn't go away. His doctor gave him medicine for the pains, but it didn't help him at all. His grandmother suggested to him that perhaps witchcraft was involved, and while Rudy did not believe her at first, he was soon so desperate he was willing to try anything.

A week after Rudy tried this spell, his neighbor across the street had a paralyzing stroke and moved away to a rest home. As soon as he did, Rudy's pains started to vanish, and three days later were gone permanently.

Coincidence? Perhaps. But Rudy B. doesn't think so.

## PROTECTING YOURSELF WITH ULTRA-MAGIC AMULETS

Of course, once you know who is using witchcraft against you, it is easy to take care of them. But what about the situation where you can't find out who it is?

In such a case, you must protect yourself with *amulets—* charms or talismans that will guard you 24 hours a day against spells and black magic, and make it impossible for them to harm you.

Ultra-Magic has made great advances in this area. In the next few pages, I am going to show you how you can construct such amulets for yourself, and reveal how to use them to best effect.

### The Ultra-Magic Coin Amulet: Ultimate Protection Against Evil

To make this amulet, you need two 25¢ pieces (the new kind,

not the silver ones) with the same date on them, a red felt-tip pen, a sheet of paper, a pair of scissors and some Scotch tape.

Take one of the quarters and lay it down on the sheet of paper. With the red pen, draw its outline. Cut the circle out of the sheet of paper on the inside of the red line, so that no red shows. Now take the red pen and draw the following on each side of the circle:

| SIDE 1 | SIDE 2 |

The meaning of these symbols is as follows:

### Side 1

The symbols used here are Alpha and Omega, the two letters that represent the Almighty. As it is said in the 21st Chapter of the *Book of Revelations,* "I am Alpha and Omega, the beginning and the end. I will give unto him that is athirst of the fountain of the water of life freely."

### Side 2

Your name should be written around the edge of the circle as shown here. The symbol in the center represents two things: the sun, and the four points of the compass. This refers to the opening of the 27th Psalm: "The Lord is my light and my salvation; whom shall I fear? The Lord is the strength of my life; of whom shall I be afraid?" The four points of the compass refer to the 24th Psalm: "The earth is the Lord's and the fulness thereof; the world, and they that dwell therein."

Take this paper circle and place it between the two quarters. The eagles on the quarters should be facing out, and should have their heads exactly opposite each other. Tape the coins together with two pieces of Scotch tape, at right angles to each other, each going around the coins twice. One piece of tape should pass straight across the body and head of the eagle.

The amulet should be consecrated on a Sunday by placing it on top of a radio which is playing a religious hymn. It should be removed promptly as soon as the hymn ends.

As long as this amulet is within 12 inches of your body, no evil spell or witchcraft has any power over you, and any spell that may already exist is instantly dissolved. Once a year, on the anniversary of the Sunday it was consecrated, the amulet must be "recharged" by placing it on top of a radio as before, on the Sunday nearest the original date.

This amulet is sometimes also called the Double-Eagle Coin Amulet. Note that each eagle is looking in a different direction, guarding you from surprise attack.

### The Ultra-Magic Quick Amulet: Fast Protection on Short Notice

The Coin Amulet is a very useful thing to have. But, as you can see, it takes time to prepare, and must be carried with you to be effective.

What can you do when you are out in public, and you feel a sudden pain, or experience a sudden disaster that seems to have been "caused?" What can you do when you see someone give you the "evil eye" or make the sign of the "horns" at you with their fingers?

For situations like these, Ultra-Magic provides fast, practical help right then and there, with this Ultra-Psychonic technique:

Simply spit once into each palm. Take your left index finger and draw a capital A on your right palm. Then take your right index finger and draw an Omega on your left palm thusly:$\Omega$. As you do this, whisper: "This is the water of life. Alpha and Omega protect me."

All evil influences will be immediately cancelled out. Unfortunately, this special Quick Amulet will protect you only until you take a drink of water. However, the amulet may be renewed immediately thereafter in the same way.

A young executive recently reported a strange experience he had with this amulet in Las Vegas. He was at a roulette table, and accidentally jostled an elderly woman. To his surprise, she pointed what looked like a rabbit's foot at him and snarled a few words in a strange language. From that moment on, he lost on every spin of the wheel. Almost down to his last dollar, he remembered the Quick Amulet and traced it on his palms. As he said the last words, "protect me," the wheel stopped directly on his number. In a short time, he had won back all his losses, and left the casino quite a few dollars ahead.

## The Ultra-Magic Home Amulet:
## How to Protect Your Worldly Goods

The preceding two amulets are fine for personal protection, but they do not protect your home and property unless you are on the spot. The Home Amulet is designed to fill this gap in your armament. It wards off and exorcises such creatures as poltergeists, fire spirits, water people and others, who may be sent to damage your home while you are away.

To make a Home Amulet, take a fully charged Double Eagle Coin Amulet and place it on top of a Bible. Then take a photograph of the Bible and amulet (you can use either regular film or Polaroid). When you have the photo, write Psalm 121 on the back of it:

> I will lift up mine eyes unto the hills, from whence cometh my
>     help.
> My help cometh from the Lord, which made heaven and earth.
> He will not suffer thy foot to be moved; he that keepeth
>     thee will not slumber.
> Behold, he that keepeth Israel shall neither slumber nor sleep.
> The Lord is thy keeper: the Lord is thy shade upon thy right
>     hand.
> The sun shall not smite thee by day, nor the moon by night.
> The Lord shall preserve thee from all evil: he shall preserve
>     thy soul.
> The Lord shall preserve thy going out and thy coming in from
>     this time forth, and even for evermore.

Next, roll the photograph up with the writing side out, until it is about the size of a cigarette. Wrap it in a piece of aluminum foil about one-half inch longer at each end. Flatten down the extra foil into a tab at each end. The foil-covered cylinder should be tacked up over the exact center of the door with two steel tacks, one at each end. As the tacks are put in, recite: "Alpha and Omega, protect me and protect my home." If there is more than one door in your home leading to the outside, a Home Amulet should be put up over each door.

## READING SIGNS AND OMENS WITH ULTRA-MAGIC

Have you ever had an advance warning that something was about to happen in your life? Have you ever noticed something out of the ordinary—a strange bird, a peculiar looking cloud, a door that suddenly stuck, odd actions by a family pet—and then, later that day, found that you had an unusually good or unusually bad experience?

Although you may not have been aware of it at the time, you had received a signal through time—a direct message from the future. It's as if a future event was casting its shadow back along the time-track, or stirring up little dust-devils, like the wind before a storm. You are experiencing an "anti-psychonic" flow.

There is a way, through Ultra-Magic, that you can spot these signs and omens and know what they mean. You can, for instance, know that a certain day is going to be a good one for you—and through knowing this, act to take fullest advantage of it.

## The Secret of the Cave

Some years ago, a Frenchman tried a new experiment. He went deep down into the ground, and set up normal living quarters in an abandoned salt mine. Everything was just as it was up on the surface—except that there were no clocks.

He was trying to find if people ran on the "natural" 24-hour cycle that has been in use since earliest times. He thought that perhaps it would turn out that people ran on a 23-hour or even a 26-hour cycle. He was way off. To his utter astonishment, he found on his return to the surface that he had been living on a *48-HOUR CYCLE!*

The experiment has been repeated by others since then, with the same results. What does it mean? Some scientists claim that it may go back to a period millions of years ago, when the earth actually rotated more slowly, at the time life was forming. Others see it as proof that man came to earth from another planet.

But Ultra-Magic researchers had another theory. They believed that the 48-hour cycle indicated that human beings had a 24-hour anti-psychonic "extension" into time—that people know exactly what is going to happen to them *at least a day before it actually takes place!*

Hard to believe? Perhaps. But these researchers conducted test after test, and when they were through, it was a proven fact. The signs and omens most people received were real, they found—although, in another sense, they actually had no existence.

In other words, the signs and omens were simply everyday occurrences—but the *act* of noticing them was significant. What this means to you is simply this: if you notice a sign or an omen, be prepared. Something different—either very good or very bad—is going to happen to you *within 24 hours.*

## How to Recognize Good and Bad Omens

As the Ultra-Magic researchers continued their tests, another fact emerged. The signs and omens that were noticed had a definite relation to the *character* of the events to come. For example, if you find a coin in the street first thing in the morning, this is a good omen, and you are going to have an excellent day. On the other hand, if you drop your coffee cup in the sink after breakfast, and it breaks, watch out—misfortune is on the way.

What about some of the other omens we mentioned, like clouds and strange birds? These must be examined more closely. For example, if a cloud takes a threatening shape—such as a knife or a hammer, this would definitely be a bad omen. A peculiar bird, on the other hand, might indicate you're about to have a good day—provided you like birds, or provided it doesn't dive at you, or make a mess on your car. The key here is *you*—what your normal reaction is. No one can tell you if anything you see is pleasant or unpleasant. Only you can decide. But once you decide—take full advantage of your knowledge. If you see a good day coming, do as much as you possibly can.

Buy a lottery ticket, for example. Start a new project. Ask your boss for a raise. Go out on a date. You simply can't lose, no matter what you do.

On the other hand, if you decide the omens are bad, pull in your horns. Sit tight. Don't commit yourself to anything. Avoid signing papers. Don't make any bets. Step softly at work, and try to avoid the boss as much as possible. Go to bed early. It's just not going to be your day.

## ULTRA-DEMONOLOGY: PROTECTION AGAINST THE FORCES OF EVIL

There is one last aspect of Ultra-Magic to be covered: defense against malignant psychic forces. Although you cannot see them, the air around you is filled with powerful beings. These invisible creatures have been known since ancient times, and called demons, spirits, elves, "little people" and many other names. Some have even been worshipped as gods by primitive man. They are inhabitants of the "Anti-Universe."

Most of the time, these invisible "demons" will not bother you. You are as hard to see for them as they are for you. But, under certain conditions, the invisible beings can be extremely dangerous. One such condition is when you are pointed out to them by an enemy, using magical means. Suddenly, you start to "glow" in front of these invisible beings like a candle in a dark room—and if the wrong "demons" are present, it can mean serious trouble for you. Imagine, for example, what might happen if one of these beings suddenly shut off your vision while you were driving a car on a busy highway at 50 miles an hour. Or if your foot "slipped" while you were going down a long flight of stairs.

Another way these beings can notice you is if you accidentally call yourself to their attention. Certain words set up vibrations that draw them—words you might accidentally use in a conversation. Certain strong emotions will attract them, too, as will certain foods, certain types of clothing and certain colors. Anything that emits anti-psychons, anti-ultrons or anti-egons is dangerous, unless shielded.

Normally, an amulet of the type we've described earlier in this chapter will be enough to protect you. But if you're not carrying one—and you don't have time to set up the Quick Amulet—you could be in serious trouble.

That is why a special sub-branch of Ultra-Magic was worked out. It is called Ultra-Demonology, and it deals with protection from the invisible creatures we've mentioned.

If you are willing to go through one rather simple "magical" ceremony, Ultra-Demonology will provide you with a Psychic Guardian for the rest of your life. This benevolent being will guard you night and day, awake or asleep, and make it impossible for invisible "demons" to attack you. Here is how to call your Guardian.

### The Ceremony That Invokes Your Psychic Guardian

On an ordinary sheet of 8½x11 white paper, draw the accompanying diagram in red ink, as carefully as possible, in the exact center.

The diagram should be exactly 4 inches in diameter.

The paper should be taken out-of-doors on a sunny day, a little before noon. The following items should be placed on the symbols underneath the Alpha and Omega signs:

In the square: a small steel needle, which has been magnetized

On the wavy lines: a drop of water

On the circle: a pure white feather, about 1/2 inch long

On the triangle: the head of an unused wooden match

Take a magnifying glass, and focus the sunlight through it to a fine point, inside the tiny central circle of the diagram, exactly at noon.

As soon as a wisp of smoke rises up from the paper, lift the magnifying glass a few inches higher so that it stops burning, and say:

> Power of Earth and Water
> Power of Air and Fire
> Alpha Omega commands you
> Act to serve my desire.

Now focus the sunlight on the matchhead lying on the triangle, and say:

> Protect me from unseen dangers
> Protect me from evil intent
> Alpha Omega commands you
> Show that you give your consent

Repeat these four lines until the matchhead bursts into

flame. Instantly stamp out the fire with your right foot, and say:

Signed, Sealed and Delivered.

From this moment on, you will have a powerful Psychic Guardian watching over you. The Guardian will protect you as long as you do not attempt to harm others by psychic means. It will stay with you all your life, if you act properly. However, if you destroy it, it is gone forever, and cannot be invoked again.

## WHAT ULTRA MAGIC CAN DO FOR YOU

Ultra-Magic is an enormously powerful tool for you to use. With its help you can:

- Make anyone into your close personal friend and helper, no matter how hostile he or she has been to you before.

- Take control of your luck and start things going your way—win at cards, numbers, the races, the market or any other activity where chance is involved.

- Attract a certain man or woman to you, arouse their romantic feelings for you and make them stay faithful as long as you choose. No matter what secret longing you have, they'll be only too happy to satisfy it.

- Blast down anyone who tries to use old-fashioned "black magic" against you, whether you know who they are or not.

- Make amulets that will protect you and your home, and keep away those who would seek to harm you.

- Defend yourself against magical attacks and curses on just a few seconds' notice.

- Discover the meaning of signs and omens that can point the way to great riches or warn you of impending disaster

- Summon up a Psychic Guardian who will protect you for life from evil psychic forces and malicious witchcraft.

## WARNING

Since Ultra-Magic is based on entirely scientific principles, it can be used for evil purposes as well as good ones. However, it is dangerous to do so. The forces involved are so much more powerful than those used in "old-fashioned" magic that they impart a negative psychonic charge to the mind of the person using them. When they are used for destructive purposes, the charge that builds up is the type that the invisible "demons" mentioned earlier are attracted to. If this occurs, there is no help available.

On the other hand, when Ultra-Magic is used for good purposes, or for self-defense, there is no danger, since the psychonic charge is a positive one. This actually *repels* the "demons."

"Good purposes" include those beneficial to yourself as well as to others. In other words, using Ultra-Magic to grow rich is a positively charged action.

"Evil purposes" are those which are designed to hurt or destroy someone who has done nothing to harm you.

So use Ultra-Magic freely, without fear or hesitation, for any good purpose. It can make you rich beyond the dreams of avarice, bring you friendship and love and protect you from those who would attack you.

# 10

## ULTRA-PROGNOSTICS:
### How
### to See into
### the Future

---

How would you like to be able to look far ahead into your future . . . to spot, well in advance, the vast opportunities, the enormous riches, the fascinating new friends and the long, healthy life that might be yours?

*You can do it* . . . with the help of Ultra-Prognostics, the mighty technique that sends your mind voyaging ahead on the River of Time, and brings it back with detailed information on what will happen in the days to come.

### Does the Future Already Exist?

For many years, this was one of the deepest and most profound questions of philosophy. Some of the greatest minds the human race has ever produced have argued on either side of the question.

But these arguments seemed to be settled permanently within the last few decades, with the discovery of the Anti-Particles and the Anti-Universe they imply.

166

For in the Anti-Universe, time must run backwards if the entire system is to function at all. And if time runs backwards, there must be a future for it to run backwards from. Thus, the age-long debate is over.

What this means to you is this: the course of your entire life has already been set. Far ahead of you down the time track stretches a long succession of days, each one already mapped out.

Or does it? Some thinkers have claimed that this is *not* the case. They say that while the future does exist, there is not just one future but many. They propose that each of these futures branches out from the present moment like the ribs of a fan.

Thus, if their theory of fan-shaped destiny is true—and I have reason to believe that it is—every moment of your life represents both a tremendous opportunity, and a tremendous danger. On the one hand, if you make a right decision, a time line opens up for you which can lead to a glorious new life. On the other hand, if you make a wrong decision, a time line opens up for you which can lead to utter disaster.

## Can the Future Be Changed?

If there is only one future, and it already exists, obviously it cannot be changed.

But if, on the other hand, there are many possible futures, then you can select the one you want by proper action in the present. In other words, your future is determined by the acts of *your own free will.*

It is my opinion that the latter situation is the true one; although at the present time, it is impossible to prove it one way or the other. I base this on the results that have been achieved with Ultra-Prognostics:

• The creation of a device that seems to reach ahead in time—the Ultronic Time-Machine—and reveal information about the future.

• The alteration of future events that seemed to be dangerous or threatening, to a more harmonious state of affairs, with this device.

• The improvement in people's personal fortunes and their increased success in their work, with the device's guidance.

• The new happiness and increased peace of mind the device has given to those who have used it.

• The correlation between the way the device works and the rest of the structure of Ultra-Psychonics.

... Or, as the old saying goes, if it looks like a duck, walks like a duck and quacks like a duck ... why, then, it must be a duck! In other words, if the effects of changing a particular action seem to result in a change in a predicted future, then *the future can be changed!*

## How Anti-Ultrons Flow Through Time

As you have seen, the existence of the Anti-Universe indicates that time must flow backwards in it. Perhaps you might like to see exactly how Anti-Ultrons flow this way. Try this experiment:

1. Imagine a man walking toward the edge of a cliff.
2. In your mind's eye, stop him at the edge.
3. Now, just as a film is reversed, reverse his actions. Step-by-step, walk him backwards from the cliff.

You have just performed your first act of Anti-Ultronic control! Notice how different this is from the act of memory.

The next step, of course, is to generate the Anti-Ultronic Laser Beam:

1. Lie down in a dark, quiet room. Close your eyes and concentrate on the field of golden light that composes the Anti-Universe.
2. Now, imagine a block or cube of grey material floating in the center of the field. This is a special kind of anti-matter—a mass of "anti-psychic atoms."
3. From the block, send out black rays in all directions, until you feel you cannot get out any more. The block is now bright yellow, almost invisible against the golden field of the Anti-Universe. It now consists of orange Anti-Egons, and green Anti-Ultrons, and is in an unstable state. Imagine a small "hole" in one face of the block.
4. Now, start the block spinning around in your mind, faster and faster, until it becomes a blur.
5. Bring the block to an instantaneous stop, with the hole lined up with the front of your forehead. A stream of bright green light rays will suddenly appear to be emerging from the hole in the block. (Actually, due to the reverse-time field, it is *entering* the hole.) This is the Anti-Ultron Laser Beam.

Practice this technique for five minutes every day until you can do it automatically, and generate the Beam in 30 seconds or less.

## Building an Ultronic Time-Machine

Once you have mastered the technique of generating the Anti-Ultron Beam, you are ready to begin construction of the Ultronic Time-Machine.

This is not really a "machine" in the conventional sense of the word, but an Ultra-Psychonic device based on the structure of the human mind and its known abilities to move through time.

It consists basically of a deck of ordinary playing cards, but these are energized, laid out and read in a special way. Gypsy fortune-tellers have used cards to predict the future for centuries, of course, but very few have ever produced dependable results. It is quite possible that the ones who did had accidentally stumbled upon the energization ritual you are about to learn:

1. Buy a brand new deck of regular playing cards. Take out the four aces and the joker, and burn them in a clean dish. Throw the ashes into running water.

2. Write down three questions on a sheet of paper. Then lie down, placing the rest of the deck of cards on your forehead.

3. Generate the Anti-Ultronic Laser Beam, and feel its green rays sweeping in through the cards, through your forehead and into the hole in the block of anti-psychic atoms. Let the rays flow through the cards for at least 15 seconds. Remove the cards and get up.

4. Next, shuffle the cards and then lay them out in piles. Make one pile for each letter of your name. For example, if your name is Walter, you would deal the cards into six piles and then restack the piles into a deck. This sensitizes the cards to your personal use. The cards should be kept in their original box when not in use, wrapped in a clean handkerchief. This will prevent their vibratory pattern from being disturbed.

5. The next step is to lay the cards out face-up on a flat surface, such as a table top, in a pattern that is seven cards wide by seven cards deep, with the central space empty. This will require exactly 48 cards, which is what you have left after burning the aces.

Page 170 shows what the pattern should look like.

The black space in the center represents the missing card.

6. Turn over the fourth card in each row, so that they are face down. This divides the cards into four distinct areas, one for each sign of the Psychonic Zodiac. The matching area for each sign is marked on the diagram.

7. The answers to your three questions are indicated by the three rows of three cards in your area. Each row contains an answer to one of the questions. Suppose the three rows look like this:

**KRIONOX**                    **VERNOX**

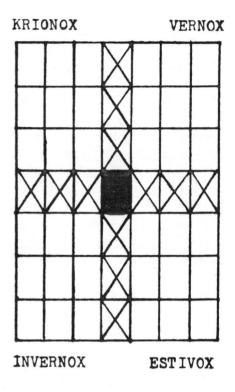

**INVERNOX**              **ESTIVOX**

(Question 1)   3D   5C   JH
(Question 2)   2C   3S   7C
(Question 3)   9H   4H   QD

(*Note:* 3D stands for the Three of Diamonds, etc.)

8. Look up each row on the chart shown on page 171, by color. Question 1, for example, contains two red cards and one black card, shown as RRB on the chart. If your sign is Krionox, RRB means "yes"; if your sign is Vernox, it means "no."

That's all there is to it—you simply lay out the cards, find the area that corresponds to your Psychonic Zodiac sign and look the results up on the chart.

### The Secret of Using Your Ultronic Time-Machine to Grow Rich

The main principle in using your Ultronic Time-Machine correctly is, of course, the careful phrasing of the questions.

Needless to say, they should be set up for a "yes" or "no" answer. But the problem lies in the wording.

Suppose, for example, you ask: "Will interest rates go up

| Color | KRIONOX: Diamonds | ESTIVOX: Hearts | VERNOX: Clubs | INVERNOX: Spades |
|-------|-------------------|------------------|----------------|-------------------|
| RRR | YES | YES | NO | NO |
| RRB | YES | YES | NO | NO |
| RBB | NO | NO | YES | YES |
| BBB | NO | NO | YES | YES |

next month?" The answer is "yes," so you decide to borrow immediately. But what you failed to ask was how long interest rates would *stay* up. They might shoot up next month, and then come down lower than they are now.

A better way to ask the question would be: "If I borrow money in the next 10 days, would this be the best deal I could get for at least six months?"

Or suppose you wanted to bet on a horse. You should not ask a question like, "Will Horse B come in first at Aqueduct tomorrow?" He might come in first—and then be disqualified.

The way to phrase the question would be, "If I bet on Horse B at Aqueduct tomorrow, will I win money on the bet?"

Suppose you wanted to make an important business decision. You might ask, "Will it be profitable to raise the price of Product C?" "Yes" replies your Ultronic Time-Machine. But you didn't ask it for how long. It might turn out to be a week—and then you lose half your customers.

A question phrased "If we raise the price of Product C, will it prove profitable over the next five years?" would give you a much more useful and definite answer.

The same care should be used to frame questions about your home life. Don't ask, "Would it be worthwhile to visit Aunt Suzy next Sunday?" The answer might be "yes"—but the problem might arise as to who the visit would be worthwhile for.

Depending on Aunt Suzy, the best way to ask the question might be "Would it be to my advantage to visit Aunt Suzy next weekend?" or perhaps, "Will Aunt Suzy be in a pleasant mood if I visit her next weekend?" or even "If I visit Aunt Suzy next weekend, will I have a safe, pleasant and rewarding trip?"

## How Brian K. Found a Fortune in Land Investment

The importance of asking the right question was recently illustrated by an experience that a friend of mine had in the real estate field. Brian K., a middle-aged office worker, was offered a chance to buy some valuable waterfront property in the southern part of New Jersey.

At that time, he had just learned about the Ultronic Time-Machine technique, and decided to see what his prospects would be if he bought the property.

"If I buy this property, will it be a profitable investment for me?" he asked.

"Yes!" replied the device, emphasizing it with three clubs, which matched his Psychonic Zodiac sign of Vernox.

Brian bought a small bungalow for $17,000, and within a year saw its value increase to over $20,000.

Another of his real estate investments recently zoomed in value from $19,400 to $32,100.

"I've found the secret of making a fortune in land investment," he recently confided to me. "It's called the Ultronic Time-Machine."

## How Nat A. Made a Killing in Commodities

With the price of almost everything on the rise these days, it's not too hard to make *some* money in the commodities market.

Nat A., however, is really striking it rich these days. He's devised a particularly clever way to use the Ultronic Time-Machine that should interest you.

Nat, you see, knows virtually nothing about commodities. But his broker does. So, once a day, Nat phones his broker and asks for his recommendations on what to buy.

That's where the Ultronic Time-Machine comes in. Before Nat gives the final word to his broker, he asks his Time-Machine, "Will the deal that Bob is offering me work out to my financial advantage?" It must work, because Nat made $30,000 profit last year.

"It's not 100% perfect," Nat admits, "because I don't really understand how the commodities market works. But when you have something like the Ultronic Time-Machine tipping you off to buy wheat at $2 a bushel and sell it at $4, it's pretty hard to lose."

## How Lionel T. Won Consistently on the Horses

Lionel T., on the other hand, understands the horses perfectly. He ought to—he's been playing them since he was a teen-ager, and he's now over 40. The trouble was, he never could seem to win until he tried the Ultronic Time-Machine.

"It works like magic," he told me recently. "I've finally gotten to the point where I think I've made back all the money I've lost over the last 30 years, and I'm starting to show a profit."

Lionel has worked out a special technique that lets him use his Ultronic Time-Machine right at the track. The secret: midget cards. You can get them in many novelty stores, or by mail from certain specialty houses. "The cards may be small, but the winnings are mighty big," says Lionel.

Since he started using them, he reports he's won consistently on the horses. He confesses, however, that he does get some strange looks from the other horse-players when they see him in action. "But," he smiles, "you should see their faces when I collect!"

## How Steve B. Spotted His Tremendous
## Future Job Prospects with a Certain Firm

Steve B., a young artist, used the Ultronic Time-Machine to solve a much more prosaic problem than which horse to bet on, although in a sense, it was really the same thing.

Steve had been out looking for a job, and was faced with the problem of deciding which of three job offers to select. None of them seemed to pay much, but Steve was just starting out, and he didn't mind working his way up from the bottom.

His first try with the Ultronic Time-Machine didn't seem to help much. "Will I get ahead if I take the job offered by Company A?" was the question he asked, and the Machine said "yes" for all three firms. Questions on raises, personality conflicts and related matters all seemed to come out even.

Then Steve B. finally hit on the key question: "Will Company A be in business five years from now?" To his surprise, only one of the three companies made the grade.

He took the job five years ago, and is now Assistant Art Director. Sad to say, the other two firms have since gone down the drain, just as the Ultronic Time-Machine predicted.

### How Rhoda J.'s Vision of New Fashions Made Her Wealthy

Women, too, have reported great success with the Ultronic Time-Machine. Take Rhoda J., for example. She was co-owner of a small, and rather unsuccessful dress business in New York City.

She decided to try the Ultronic Time-Machine, after she had heard about it, to predict such things as skirt lengths and clothing styles. While most of the other dress makers were bringing out the midi, Rhoda J.'s firm just ignored it. Later on, they expanded their line of jeans and denim clothes to catch the peak of the demand.

In a very short time, Rhoda J.'s vision of new fashions made her firm's profits move out of the red and into the black, and she is now a very wealthy woman.

Her technique was somewhat similar to Nat A.'s; although, unlike him, she knows her business backwards and forwards. However, she, too, depended on the experts. She followed the fashion scene very closely, attended fashion shows and carefully read the leading publications.

Before she made a fashion decision, however, she would ask her Ultronic Time-Machine, "Will my company show a profit on this line if we bring it out next season?" As you can see, she certainly got the right answers!

### The Secret of Using Your Ultronic Time-Machine for Power Over Others

This demonstrates how your Ultronic Time-Machine can be used to give you definite "yes" and "no" answers to a wide variety of questions. The same technique can be extended to increasing your power and influence over others.

If, for example, you want a man or woman to do something for you, you can simply ask your Time-Machine, "Is tomorrow the best day to ask (name) for (the favor you want)?" If the Machine says "yes," you can further refine the time right down to the very hour and minute that would be the best time to ask. If it says, "no," you can use other questions to find the best week, or the best month, and then focus down on the right day and time again.

To increase the sensitivity of the results, you can try placing a photo of the person you're trying to influence right in the center of the Ultronic Time-Machine, which as you may recall, has an empty central space. Naturally, the photo must be a small one, as it should not touch or cover any of the other cards.

Since you can ask three questions at a time, you can see that pinpointing the right time to ask can be done very rapidly. You can also ask other questions to discover a person's likes and dislikes, their secret beliefs and what they presently think about you and other people. This gives you enormous power over them, because you have "inside information" on what they're going to do before they even know it themselves!

### How Anna G. Spots Her Future
### Friends and Enemies

Anna G., a middle-aged actress I know, uses this technique to great effect in her theater life. Her career in the entertainment world depends, to a great extent, on her contacts with agents, producers, directors and wealthy patrons of the arts. From almost complete obscurity, she has risen rapidly in her profession and has already won starring roles in two off-Broadway shows.

Her questions are all aimed at this goal. "Will (name) help me or hinder me in my career?" she asks her Time-Machine, and guides her actions accordingly. Her steady rise toward the top indicates that she's certainly getting the right answers!

### How Leonard G. Gets His Way with People
### by Knowing Their Futures

Leonard G., on the other hand, uses his Ultronic Time-Machine purely for his own personal pleasure. I sometimes regret having shown him the technique, as I am sorry to say that he has not been using it for very worthwhile purposes.

At parties, for example, he uses it to pick out the most likely young girls to take home with him. "Will (name) come up to my apartment tonight?" he asks, using a special midget deck that he pretends to do card tricks with. His card tricks never seem to work, but he makes out quite well otherwise.

Leonard G., as you can see, is a somewhat shady character. He doesn't seem to have a job, but he always has plenty of money and drives around in a fancy new car. It's too bad that he uses the powers of the Ultronic Time-Machine for such selfish ends, but it is, after all, only a tool.

If you suspect someone is using an Ultronic Time-Machine to take advantage of you, there is a very easy way to protect yourself. Simply carry your own Ultronic Time-Machine cards with you at all times. The anti-ultronic field that surrounds your Machine will tend to block out penetration of your future by anyone else.

### The Secret of Using Your Ultronic Time-Machine for Better Health and Longer Life

One really worthwhile use of your Ultronic Time-Machine is the improvement of your health.

"How can this be done?" you ask. There are a number of ways. Suppose you take vitamin pills, for example, but do not want to take them every day. "Is it safe to skip my vitamin pills today?" you might ask your Time-Machine every morning. Or you might even ask it if you should take some vitamins and not others. "Should I take an extra Vitamin C pill this morning?" you might ask.

Now, of course, there is more to good health than just taking vitamins. Here, too, your Ultronic Time-Machine can help you in such things as deciding exactly which foods to eat for a balanced diet, what kinds of exercise to take and how to avoid situations in which you may be exposed to disease or infection.

Needless to say, if you should become seriously ill, you should consult your doctor immediately, without waiting to consult your Time-Machine or anything else.

You can, of course, use your regular deck of Ultronic Time-Machine cards for health purposes, but there is a way to prepare a specially sensitized deck, if you'd like to do so. Using a clean needle, prick your thumb, and rub a small streak of blood across the top edge of a new deck of cards. Then, proceed as before. Keep this deck separate from the others—this Ultronic Time-Machine should only be used to help you improve your health and extend your lifespan.

## How Catherine O. Avoids Accidents
## and Infections

An elderly relative of mine uses her Ultronic Time-Machine purely as a preventive device. Before she takes a trip or goes to any place where she will come into contact with large numbers of people, she asks her Machine, "Will I return safe and in good health from this trip?"

Silly? Perhaps. But she has managed to avoid a few rather nasty auto accidents, a bus crash and an airplane disaster. And, over the past four years, she hasn't had as much as a sniffle each winter. How many of us can say the same?

## How Raymond P. Cured a Serious Illness
## with Medicine from the Future

A friend of mine, Raymond P., swears that his Ultronic Time-Machine saved his life—in a very unusual way.

About a year ago, he developed what he thought was just a very bad cold. He considered going to see a doctor, but felt it probably wouldn't be necessary. To be sure, he asked his Ultronic Time-Machine, "If I see a doctor next week, will I be all right?"

To his surprise, the answer was a definite "no!" Ray decided not to take a chance, and saw his family doctor immediately. The doctor found that he had a rapidly developing case of pneumonia—and gave him an antibiotic immediately. His ailment cleared up rapidly, and he was back to normal in a week or so.

"It's lucky you saw me when you did," his doctor told him, "or you might have been in the hospital for quite a while."

Ray realized just how lucky he'd been when he looked in a medical book and discovered that while 19 out of 20 people recover from pneumonia with proper medical treatment, pneumonia used to kill one in every three or four people it attacked!

In effect, his life had been saved by medicine from the future. Had he followed his original inclination, he would not have seen a doctor until the following week—and that might have been much too late.

Did Raymond P. actually change his future? Did he pick a different path along the fan-shaped destiny that lay before him? Decide for yourself.

## The Secret of Using Your Ultronic Time-Machine
## for a More Exciting Love Life

Is your romantic life everything you want it to be? Does the person you care for respond the way you want?

Your Ultronic Time-Machine can give you powerful help in this department!

There are a number of questions you can ask that will definitely smooth your way and make things better for you. But, before you ask them, I strongly suggest you sit down and read through a good marriage manual. This will open up your eyes to a great many possibilities that you might not be aware of.

Next, ask your questions in a step-by-step manner. First, find out what will please your loved one most. "If I wear this garment, will (name) find me more attractive tomorrow night?" you might ask. Check out every detail—what to wear, what to talk about, what to avoid, where to go, when to "close in" and so on.

Once you've gotten the other party definitely interested, then apply what you've learned from the marriage manual. "If I do (thus and so) will (name) like it?" you might ask. Work out a definite campaign, starting out with simple, introductory things and moving slowly up to whatever level of activity you desire.

Your Time-Machine will guide you every step of the way, revealing just what to do and how and when to do it.

To "sensitize" your Time-Machine especially for love and romance, place two photos in the empty central space: yours and your loved one's. Your photo should always be placed on top of the other.

## How Edgar O. Spotted His Future Wife

A young college student I know used this Ultronic Love Technique to find, woo and win the young lady of his choice.

He had been invited, along with the rest of the student body, to a wide variety of different club activities on the first night of the term. "Will I meet the girl of my dreams if I go to Club A's meeting?" he asked. "No," said his Time-Machine, and he gradually worked his way through the entire list of clubs, until he hit a definite "yes" reply.

Edgar already had a pretty good idea of the kind of girl he was looking for, but he used his Time-Machine to confirm each detail. His Machine suggested he look for a tall blonde in a red dress, about an hour after he arrived.

He was a little disappointed when he first got there, as no one seemed to fit the description his Machine had given him. Suddenly, about an hour later, he looked up and the exact girl the

Machine had forecast was standing in front of him. "Do you have a match?" she asked . . . and Edgar took it from there.

He found her to be everything he had been hoping for, and more. Two months later, they were married, and are one of the happiest couples I know.

## How Dolores S. Found Out Her Future Children's Sex

A very popular use of the Ultronic Time-Machine a few years back was forecasting the sex of unborn children. Today, of course, medical science can tell you this almost from the day of conception.

However, medical science will never catch up with the Ultronic Time-Machine in one respect: predicting the sex of future children *before* they're conceived.

Dolores S., for example, particularly wanted a daughter, and used her Ultronic Time-Machine to weed out her suitors until she found the man her Machine predicted would give her a daughter. She married him, and the prediction came true. Amusingly, she's now had *three* daughters and is hoping for a son.

## Other Time-Machine Uses

There are, of course, many, many other uses of your Ultronic Time-Machine, too many to cover here. Ask the right questions, and your machine will tell you:

- Where to take your vacation
- Which furniture to buy
- Which groups to join
- Which house to live in
- Which diet to try
- Which job to do first
- Which gifts to give
- Who to vote for
- Which doctor to visit
- Which car to drive
- Which pet to select
- Which school to attend
- Which clothes to wear
- What career to pursue

. . . and how to solve a host of other problems.

You can even use it as an extra way to strengthen and develop your psychic powers, particularly your ability to see into the future. For example, you can use it in conjunction with a crystal ball or Ouija board, as a separate check on the accuracy of their results. Once you get the "feel" of predicting the future, once you establish a flow of Anti-Ultrons from your mind into the time dimension, you will discover that other prophecy devices are easier to operate and give more accurate results.

It's like learning to drive a car. Once you learn how to drive a Ford, you can quickly and easily learn to drive a Chevvy or an Oldsmobile.

Don't be afraid to ask your Ultronic Time-Machine for help in solving your problems. It will not wear out or grow weaker—on the contrary, the more you use it, the stronger and more reliable it will get.

## WHAT ULTRA-PROGNOSTICS CAN DO FOR YOU

In this chapter, you've seen:

- How it is possible to change the future by means of the theory of fan-shaped destiny.

- How Anti-Ultrons flow backwards through time, and how you can use this knowledge to generate an Anti-Ultronic Laser Beam.

- How to build an Ultronic Time-Machine for less than a dollar, and use it to look ahead into the future.

- How to use your Ultronic Time-Machine to acquire various kinds of wealth such as real estate, good-salaried jobs, tips on the horses, guidance on investments and "inside" business secrets.

- How to use your Ultronic Time-Machine to gain power over others.

- How to discover your secret friends and enemies, with its help.

- How to enjoy improved health and greater security by "sensitizing" a special "health deck" to your bodily functions.

- How to find a more thrilling and pleasurable love life with the guidance of a specially prepared Ultronic Time-Machine.

- How to use your Ultronic Time-Machine to increase and heighten your psychic powers.

... Here, in short, is a simple, safe, fast and accurate way to predict future events and make them turn out the way you want them to.

# 11

## ULTRA-NUMEROLOGY:
### How to Control
### the Mystic Numbers
### That Rule Your Life

---

The next time you're in a department store, see if you can get to try one of the new electronic calculators. It's really fascinating. You push a few buttons, and suddenly a little screen lights up and rows of numbers start to march across it. It's almost as if they had a life of their own!

Maybe they do. For many thousands of years, man has believed in the influence and power of numbers on his life, and with good reason.

### How Your Life Is Ruled by Numbers

"Can this be true?" you ask. "How do numbers control my life?"

Look around you. If someone wants to phone you, they dial—a number. If you deposit money in your bank account, it is deposited to—a number. Zip codes, Social Security numbers, charge accounts, auto license plates, the house you live in, every one controlled by—a number.

Do the numbers matter? If you don't think so, try using a wrong one.

Yes, in some ways, numbers are our masters. But there are ways to use this knowledge—to put the mighty power of numbers to work for you—to guide you and help you, and make things go more smoothly. In this chapter, you'll see how the centuries-old secrets of number magic are not just mumbo-jumbo, but actually represent a whole range of abstract forces I call Ultra-Numerology.

You're about to discover how to use the hidden power of the numbers in your life consciously, for the first time. You're about to "tune in" on the key numbers that will guide you toward wealth and happiness. And it's all going to start . . . *now!*

### What Numbers Really Mean Psychonically

In Chapter 5, you may recall, you discovered that the brain works on an off/on basis. Everything, including numbers, is stored in it as an electric charge, either plus or minus.

Later on, you saw that for every Psychon there is an Anti-Psychon, for every Ultron an Anti-Ultron and for every Egon an Anti-Egon.

In other words, every number in your brain, every surge of Ultra-Psychonic power is measured in binary terms. There are no 2's, 3's, 4's, 5's or 6's—there are only quantities expressed in 1's and 0's—1, 10, 11, 100, 101, 110 and so on.

This means that you are really *free* of the tyranny of numbers on the mental and Ultra-Psychonic levels. It means that you have no "built-in" number buttons that can be pushed by outside events to control you. And, above all, it means that *you* have the capacity to turn things around and use numbers to direct your destiny—by using the techniques of Ultra-Numerology.

### How to Start Using Numbers to Control Your Future

Where do you start? The first step, obviously, is to see if the problem can be simplified. Are we looking for a dozen numbers or half a dozen? Or is there just one Master Number that rules them all?

Take an imaginary Peter Brown, for example. He might live at 3214 Apple Drive, have a phone number of 555-1212 and drive a car with the license EJO-7819. Is there one unifying number in this collection of seemingly random digits?

And if there were, how could Peter Brown use this number to his advantage?

You're going to see that there *is* one number buried in the mass of facts above—the Ultra-Psychonic Number (or UP-Number, for short) that connects each item to the others. Then you're going to see what your own UP-Number is, and how to use it.

## How to Find Your Master "UP-Number"

The first step in finding your Ultra-Psychonic Number is a simple one: write your name on a piece of paper and count the letters. In the example we used, you would write:

           PETER        BROWN
           1 2 3 4 5    1 2 3 4 5

Then you add the letters for each name together: $5 + 5 = 10$. Since UP-Numbers run only from 1 to 9, any number over nine must be broken into its component numbers and added again: $1 + 0 = 1$.

*This is Peter Brown's Master UP-Number: 1.*

Furthermore, he has a secondary UP-Number, 5, since each of his names have 5 letters. (Many people have two secondary numbers, if their first and last names have different numbers of letters.)

Let's see how this fits the data we have on Peter Brown:

*Address:*   3214 Apple Drive
            $3+2+1+4 = 10 = 1 + 0 = 1$
            *Apple* has 5 letters, as does *Drive*. Again, the same pattern.

*Phone:*     555-1212
            Note the pattern of fives and ones.

*Auto License:*   EJO-7819
            $7+8+1+9 = 25$, which is 5 times 5.
            E is the fifth letter of the alphabet, J is the tenth and O is the fifteenth. Again, a pattern of fives and ones.

Now, try it yourself. Figure out your own Master UP-Number and your secondary numbers. See how it fits your own personal data. You'll be amazed at the pattern that develops!

"But," you say, "some numbers don't seem to fit." Obviously not. If all your numbers fit your Master UP-Number pattern, you'd be living quite a different kind of life—a life much richer and fuller than you do now. The more numbers in your life that conflict with your basic pattern, the more problems you have.

I believe it!" you say. "My numbers are all fouled up, and my life is not what I want it to be at all. But what can I do? Can I change my numbers?"

Sometimes you can. Your address, for example, can be changed by moving. Your phone number can be changed just by asking the phone company to do so, and paying a small fee. Even your auto license plates can be changed, in some states, if you pay for it.

But some other numbers are not so easy to change. Your Social Security number is a hard one, for example. Even if you get a new one, your old one still stays on the books.

A really drastic solution, of course, is to change your name legally. But this usually creates so many other problems that it isn't advisable. Women have a great advantage here—they can change their last name by marriage.

## How to Use Your UP-Number to Spot Friendly People

The easiest and quickest use of your UP-Number is to spot people who will tend to be friendly toward you.

Write their name on a piece of paper and figure out their UP-Number. For instance, Oscar Smith would tend to be friendly toward Peter Brown, since they are both on the same "wavelength," so to speak.

There are also friendly vibrations from numbers which are related to yours. If your UP-Number was 6, for example, you would also get a friendly response from people with UP-Numbers of 2 or 3, since 2 x 3 equals 6.

However, this system has one drawback. If you run across someone who is not living in harmony with his UP-Number pattern, he is likely to have so many problems that he isn't friendly toward *anyone*. I'm sure you've met a few people like that. In some cases, if you keep trying, you can even manage to become friendly with this type, but it will take quite a bit of time and effort.

## How Leo M. Got a $100,000 Loan from His UP-Number Twin

Leo M. scoffed at the UP-Number idea when he talked to me

about a year ago, but he's a firm believer now. Head of a small business, he was having trouble getting the necessary capital for a major expansion of his firm.

"Try it," I urged him. "You have nothing to lose, and everything to gain."

Since Leo's first name had three letters, and his last name had six, his UP-Number was 9. "Look for another 9," I said.

To his surprise, the only 9 around was one of the toughest, crustiest bankers in town. "He'll never lend me a nickel, " he groaned.

But Leo was desperate. Knowing what he had to overcome, he put extra time into preparing and refining his loan request. He even managed to get an appointment on the ninth of the month at 9 a.m. Did it work? "Like a charm," Leo reported. "He even offered to lend me more than I asked for."

## How to Use Your UP-Number to Select the Right Location

Let's suppose you're not satisfied with your present address and want to move. How should you do it?

Assuming other factors are equal, there are three things you should take into account:

1. The new street address

2. The city and state

3. Your new zip code

You've already seen how to figure out the number pattern for a street address. Remember that perfection may not always be possible, however, and that sometimes you can get the right number but not the right street name, and vice versa. Even a partial pattern will help make your new home a harmonious place.

Your new zip code's number pattern is also easy to calculate. Simply add up the numbers in the zip code until you get a number between 1 and 9, as you have done previously.

The same is true of your city and state. For example, if you were going to move to Chicago, Illinois, the city has seven letters and the state has eight. Thus, the total would be 15, or 1 + 5. The location would therefore be favorable to people with UP-Numbers of 6, and to a lesser extent, to people with UP-Numbers of 1 or 5.

Of course, location is not everything. It affects your life to a certain extent, but it also affects the lives of thousands of people around you. The closer the number is to your everyday life, the more important it is. Thus, your street address is more important than your zip code, and your zip code is more important than your city and state, in terms of the effect of their number patterns.

### How Sally L. Found the Home of Her Dreams in Just One Week

Sally L., a former neighbor, thinks quite highly of selecting a house location by UP-Number. Her UP-Number was 2, and she was quite unhappy at an address I shall call 567 Main Street. She had a wet basement, termites and a constant stream of cars past her door.

Finally, she decided to move, but she just couldn't seem to find the right house, although she went around with real estate people for months, looking at place after place.

Visiting me one evening, she asked what the calculations I was working on were. I explained about UP-Number patterns, and Sally was quite intrigued, although her husband pooh-poohed the whole thing.

The next weekend, before the real estate salesman took her and her husband to see anything, she looked over the list of prospects and selected the one that had the "right" number pattern in its address. To her surprise, it turned out to be exactly what she and her husband had been looking for. They closed the deal that very day, and have been living there very happily for over five years now.

"It's the house I always dreamed about, and never could find," she told me.

### How to Choose the Best Time for Any Action with Your UP-Number

You saw a little while ago how Leo M. got the loan he wanted not only by finding his UP-Number twin, but also by setting up an appointment at a date and time that tied in with the same number.

Naturally, it's not always possible to set the date or get an appointment at the time you want. But there *are* ways you can use to activate your UP-Number vibrations.

As you may recall, Leo M.'s UP-Number was 9. If he could not have gotten the appointment time he wanted, he could have tried arriving nine minutes early. Or, assuming the only appointment he could get was in the afternoon, he could have tried phoning the banker at 9 a.m.

To prove to yourself that your UP-Number really influences your life, try this experiment: Select the next day of the month that is connected with your UP-Number, and see what comes to you in the mail on that day. For example, if your UP-Number is 4, see what the mailman brings you on the 4th, 13th, 22nd or 31st of the month. You'll be pleasantly surprised!

Naturally, when you *can* control the date for a particular action, the results will be much more impressive. For example, if you decide to buy a car and your UP-Number is 3, you'll really get a winner if you can manage to make your selection at 3:33 p.m. on March 3rd. Should this day happen to fall on the third day of the week, the vibratory influences will be even more strongly in your favor.

However, watch out for negative number influences. An aggressive salesman with a strong 5 bias might, in the case we were just talking about, overcome your number plan by stretching out the buying process, and stick you with a lemon. Be on your guard.

### How Terry A. Struck It Rich
### on Wall Street

The effectiveness of this technique increases as the timing control becomes more precise. For someone like Terry A., who speculates in the stock market, it's like a dream come true. His UP-Number is 8, and he plays it to the hilt.

He phones his broker only at eight minutes after the hour, buys stock in 800-share lots and tries to work as many 8's into his buying and selling operations as he possibly can.

When I first met him, he was living in a sleazy slum apartment in the Bronx. His magic 8's must be working for him, because he's now living in a penthouse on Park Avenue and has a summer home in the Caribbean.

### How Your UP-Number Can Guide You
### to Overlooked Opportunities

All around you, on every hand, lies a vast sea of untapped opportunities—a surging ocean of ways to make extra money, to meet fabulous new people and win them to your side, to seize and enjoy a glorious new kind of life that most people do not even suspect exists.

As the Lord parted the Red Sea for the hosts of Israel, so can your UP-Number open a path for you into the Promised Land of prosperity and happiness.

Use your UP-Number in every way that you can. If it is 7, then live a 7-oriented life. Wake up at 7 a.m. Eat seven different things for breakfast. Or suppose it is 1. Wake up at one minute after your usual hour. Eat one slice of toast. Drink one cup of coffee. And so on.

But, above all, put yourself in harmony with your UP-Number. If it is 8, carry eight coins in your wallet. Or six coins, if 6 is your number. A woman whose UP-Number is 3, for example, can wear a pin with a three-pointed piece of jewelry on it. A man whose number is 4 can carry a handkerchief folded into four parts. If nothing else is available, just write your UP-Number on a piece of paper and carry it around in your pocket.

Watch the doors swing open! Watch a golden cascade of wealth and power come surging out into your life! Watch a miracle of joy and fulfillment become yours at last!

But be alert. Listen for the number-message that applies to you. If your UP-Number is 5, and you see a bargain for $5, grab it. If you play the numbers, pick variations and combinations of 5 on your lucky days. Buy five lottery tickets at a time.

Suppose you enter a contest, and your UP-Number is 6. Submit six entries. Write a 6 on each envelope under the stamp. Mail three entries off at 6 a.m., 6:06 a.m., 6:36 a.m., and the other three at 6 p.m., 6:06 p.m. and 6:36 p.m.

Use your UP-Number to help you develop your other Ultra-Psychonic powers, too. For example, when you get ready to start practicing a particular technique, try to tie it in to one of your harmonious number-hours. Repeat it, unless otherwise instructed, the same amount of times as your UP-Number.

Sometimes your UP-Number signal may not be obvious. You saw how the license plate letters EJO carried a hidden message of 5's and 1's. So, too, a person's name may appear to lack the crucial digits and yet still contain them. Examine names, words and combinations of letters very closely. Measure things, if you can, and see how many feet or inches they are. Weigh them, if there's no other means of finding out. Be certain—make sure— check and double-check!

But when your number-signal comes, whether it be straight

numbers, letters or anything else—even clouds in the sky or the number of birds in a tree—be prepared to act!

## How Ralph W. Made the Car Buy
## of His Life

A young office worker I know recently used this principle to get himself a tremendous buy in a used car. Just starting out in the business world, he could not afford a new car, and so answered several ads in the local newspaper for used ones.

He finally narrowed his choice down to two cars: one offered by an elderly woman who obviously was unable to do much driving, and one offered by a young man of about his own age. The two cars seemed to be very similar in terms of physical condition, age and mileage.

Ralph was about to take the old woman's offer when he noticed her license plate: it was all 7's. His UP-Number was 9. Ralph checked the other car offered—its license contained the digits 909. He decided to follow his number-signal and bought the second car.

A week or so later, he heard that the old woman's late husband had been a traveling salesman, and the mileage figure really needed 100,000 miles added to it.

Meanwhile, the car he bought turned out to be a real prize. The former owner had been an engineering student, and not only had maintained it in tip-top condition, but had even added a few improvements that gave it much better gas mileage and a smoother ride.

## Secrets of the Power Primes

You may remember from your math class days that a prime number is one that cannot be divided by anything else. Thus 1, 2, 3, 5 and 7 are primes, while 4, 6, 8 and 9 are not.

What this means to you is this: if your UP-Number is not a prime—if it is 4, 6, 8 or 9—you can get help from the factors that make it up. Thus, 4 can be broken down into 2 times 2, 6 can be broken down into 2 times 3, 8 can be broken down into 2 times 4 and 9 can be broken down into 3 times 3.

Suppose that your UP-Number is 9, but you are in a situation where you must choose between several numbers other than 9. Since your UP-Number cannot be applied, you must fall back on the

Power Primes that make it up. In this case, your best bet would obviously be number 3.

"But," you say, "suppose my UP-Number had been 6 or 7?"

If your UP-Number had been 7, your chances of making the best choice among the alternatives would not have been very good—unless, of course, you could manage to work a 7 into the time element.

On the other hand, had your UP-Number been 6, you would have two Power Primes to choose from: 2 and 3. Either one would probably be favorable, and if you could manage to reinforce it with a timing signal, your chances would be greatly improved. The advantage here over the previous situation is this: 7 would limit you to just one number to work with, while 6 would give you three timing numbers: 2, 3 and 6. If, for some reason, you couldn't make your selection at 2:00 p.m., you could also try 2:02, 2:03 and 2:06.

### How Roger B. Broke the Bank at Las Vegas

A friend of mine recently reported to me that she saw this system in action in Las Vegas, where a gambler practically cleaned out one of the casinos by using one basic number and its factors, over and over, at a roulette wheel.

Of course, as his winnings started to pile up, the casino finally put a limit on them—which he quickly reached. So, you might say, insofar as it is possible, he "broke the bank" at Las Vegas.

This brings up an interesting point. Some people—gamblers, particularly—have an almost instinctive understanding of Ultra-Numerology without ever having read one word about it. It should be interesting to see what happens when its principles are more widely known and scientifically applied.

### Triads and Squares: How to Pick
### Team Members Who Work Together Best

In many fields—business, sports, politics, home life—there are things that only teams can do. There are baseball nines, business departments, families, clubs, political tickets—all consisting of three or more people.

Can Ultra-Numerology help in putting together a winning team in these areas? The answer is a resounding "yes!"

There are several ways such a team can be assembled. Here are some successful patterns you can use:

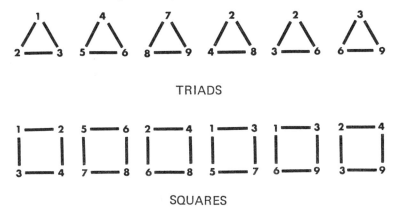

TRIADS

SQUARES

If you can match the UP-Numbers of your team members in any of the patterns shown above, you have the basis for the strongest possible team you can get.

By combining the triads and squares, you can put together teams of 3, 4, 6, 7, 8, 9 and more people.

The only team setup not covered by this arrangement is teams of 5. These can, however, be arranged as follows:

1━2━3━4━5    5━6━7━8━9    1━3━5━7━9    2━4━5━6━8

Note that every arrangement must contain the key number 5.

Picking pairs of people has already been covered in this chapter earlier under the section on how to spot friendly people, but to recap the technique briefly, you should match people who either have identical UP-Numbers or whose UP-Numbers are connected through Power Prime factors.

## How Adam L. Assembled a Winning
## Little League Team

A losing Little League team in a nearby town was recently invigorated by some drastic changes in its membership. The coach, Adam L., although he did not know about Ultra-Numerology, certainly seems to have employed its principles.

According to reports in a local newspaper, nearly half the team was dropped, and new players brought in. At the time, purely as an exercise, I checked out the names of the players on both the old and new teams. I was not surprised to find that the UP-Number distribution on the old team made it impossible to arrange the nine players into any favorable combination of triads.

The new team names, on the other hand, fell neatly into a 1-2-3, 2-4-8, 3-6-9 combination. Since the changeover, the new team has been winning game after game, and seems to be a strong contender for the local area pennant.

### Using UP-Numbers with Ultra-Divination

One area of Ultra-Psychonics that responds particularly well to the use of the UP-Number technique is Ultra-Divination. There are at least four ways you can improve your results with it:

1. Timing, of course, is the most obvious way. If you have not been getting clearcut results with your Psychonic Radar Locator, try using it at a time that's numerically "right" for you.

2. Another helpful technique is Digital Repetition. If moving your Psychonic Radar Locator over a map or through an area does not give you a strong response to what you're looking for, repeat the process as many times as your UP-Number would indicate.

3. Instead of using just one object for the pendulum on your Psychonic Radar Locator, use a number of objects equal to your UP-Number. For example, if you're looking for oil, and your UP-Number is 7, fill seven small bottles with oil, put them all in a plastic bag and use the entire bag as the weight for the pendulum.

4. If you are using the Summoning Chant, repeat it the exact number of times of your UP-Number.

Naturally, these are not the only ways you can use your UP-Number with Ultra-Divination. However, these are the four most effective ones.

### UP-Numbers and Advice from the Bible

A correspondent recently wrote me from the West Coast about a new and fairly unusual way to use your UP-Number to get advice and help in moments of stress.

Here is the technique he has devised:

1. Clearly state your question or problem on a sheet of paper.

2. Let your Bible fall open at random, and put your finger on the page.

3. Count down paragraphs equal to your UP-Number from the top of the page. Start counting from the first whole paragraph.

4. Read the final paragraph, and see if it gives you guidance.

5. Repeat the process the same number of times as your UP-Number.

Suppose, for example, you are having marital troubles, and want to know what to do to bring your spouse back to you. If your UP-Number was 2, you might open the Bible and find the following verses:

I was dumb with silence, I held my peace, even from good; and my sorrow was stirred. *Psalms 39:2*

Moreover, if thy brother shall trespass against thee, go and tell him his fault between thee and him alone: if he shall hear thee, thou hast gained thy brother. *Matthew 18:15*

You might interpret this to mean that you should say nothing to your erring spouse, but that you should seek out the one who is causing the trouble and try to make him or her see the error of his or her ways.

Of course, not all Bible messages are crystal clear at first. You should ponder over them for at least a day or so, before taking any action. Do nothing hastily.

Two final points: First of all, it does not make any difference which Bible you use, as long as it is the book of your faith. Secondly, you will *never* get a message this way that will advise you to do anything illegal or sinful. If you think you have received such a message, you should examine it more closely until its true meaning is revealed.

## WHAT ULTRA-NUMEROLOGY CAN DO FOR YOU

In this chapter, you've seen:

- How numbers control most of the events in your life.

- How to figure out your master UP-Number.

- How your UP-Number can be used to find people who will be friendly and sympathetic toward you.

- How your UP-Number can help you find the ideal place for you to live.

- How your UP-Number can point out the best time to undertake any action that you want to succeed.

- How to use your UP-Number to win contests and cash in on other "luck-controlled" opportunities.

- How your UP-Number can help you develop your other Ultra-Psychonic powers to realize your full Ultra-Psychonic potential.

- How to use Power Primes to help you in situations where you cannot use your main UP-Number.

- How to use Ultra-Numerological *triads* and *squares* to put together teams that will be the most effective and harmonious.

- How to make your Ultra-Divination techniques work more effectively by coordinating them with your UP-Number.

- How to get guidance from the Bible on many pressing personal and business problems through the use of your UP-Number.

The more you study Ultra-Numerology, the more you will be convinced that it really works. Put it to work for you now!

# 12

## ULTRA-TELEPATHY:

### How to Probe
### the Most Intimate Secrets
### of Others

For several weeks George D. had been trying to become friendly with Lucy, the new secretary in his office. But because he was only a junior clerk, she had been very snooty toward him. He figured she was after bigger game. Today, though, was going to be different. Today, he was going to try Ultra-Telepathy—an unusual technique a friend of his had discovered and taught to him the evening before.

"Good morning, Lucy," he said as she came in, "have a nice evening?"

"Oh hi George," she said, "I had a fabulous evening." But George could see that she was *really* thinking, "What a lie. I had a lousy evening, all alone again, just watching TV."

"What would you like to do tonight?" he asked.

"I'm going to be very busy," she replied, the way she always did. Only this time George knew she was thinking, "Real busy. Staring at the TV again. What I'd really like to do would be to go dancing. But who'd ask me?"

"How would you like to go dancing, Lucy?" he asked. "It just so happens I have two free tickets to the Firemen's Ball." (He didn't really have them—but he knew where he could buy them after work.)

"Gee, George, I'd like to..." she said, "but I have a big date." George heard her thinking, "I wish I did. I'd go out with George, even, but he'd probably take me to a hamburger stand for dinner... he looks like he hasn't got a dime."

"Sorry to hear that, Lucy," said George, "I know a great little place called The Roost, with the most delicious T-bone steaks you ever tasted. And there's still time to make a reservation."

Needless to say, George got the date. And he soon found he could get one anytime he wanted, even if it was only a date to go bird-watching. He had Lucy wrapped around his little finger—because he always knew exactly what she wanted.

## The Amazing Power of Ultra-Telepathy

George was able to read Lucy like a book—he knew her most intimate, private thoughts just as if she were whispering them in his ear—because he had mastered the incredible technique of Ultra-Telepathy. This fantastic power is about to be yours.

What it means to you is this:

- You can read the mind of anyone, man or woman, young or old, friend or enemy.

- You can know the innermost thoughts of people sitting right next to you, or a thousand miles away—even over the telephone.

- You can send telepathic messages to anyone, even perfect strangers, no matter how near or far.

- You can erect an impenetrable shield around your mind that ordinary telepathy cannot get through.

- You can send your thoughts through time and contact the greatest minds of the past and future.

- You can even reach out into interstellar space and contact beings on other worlds millions of light-years away!

I think you'll agree that Ultra-Telepathy is as different from ordinary telepathy as a grapefruit is from a raisin. Best of all, you can master it in just one evening, without any equipment or training. Once you do so, it becomes an automatic ability—as easy to use as your fingers—and always at your beck and call.

## SECRET OF THE ULTRA-TELEPATHIC POWER GLOBE

To learn the knack of Ultra-Telepathy, you need just one thing: a quiet place to practice, where you can lie down. Close your eyes.

Once you have done this, let your mind go completely blank. Think of the inside of your head as being filled with a black, murky fog. Now, try to visualize a tiny point of golden light right in the center of it. You are looking at a "psychic atom"!

Next, start to expand this point of light into a small globe of golden light the size of a pea. Hold it that size for a few seconds . . . then let it start to grow again until it fills the entire inside of your head. Your mind is now emitting a beam of psychons.

The inner light you are now seeing is called the Ultra-Telepathic Power Globe. There is NO LIMIT to its power.

The next step is to expand the Power Globe outside of your head. Simply imagine that it is filling the room—and it will do so. You have now achieved Stage One—the ability to read the innermost thoughts of anyone within the room the Globe is filling.

### Stage One—How to Read Nearby Thoughts

Practice expanding the Power Globe from a tiny point until it fills the room, over and over. After a while, you will notice that the brightness that fills the room is as strong as the original point of light—and the original point of light is almost as bright as a star. This is called *reinforcement,* and it is the secret behind Ultra-Telepathy.

Next, start a conversation with someone you know—and while you are talking, expand the Power Globe to room size. Observe him or her closely while you do this—you will notice that they become strangely jumpy and uneasy. This means you are starting to penetrate their mind. Try to guess what he or she is going to say next. Soon you'll discover that you can predict every word they say, before they open their mouth. The next step is to read their hidden thoughts—the ones they never say aloud. Concentrate on the golden Power Globe. Concentrate—and you will feel their secret thoughts start to reveal themselves. Subconsciously, the person you are talking to will sense your mind probe. He or she will start to invent excuses to leave—anything to get away before their innermost secrets are laid bare.

Karen D. saved her life this way. For some months, a young man named Howard B. had been urging her to go out with him. She was starting to weaken when she learned the secret of the Power Globe. She tried it on Howard the very next day—and was so shocked she could barely leave fast enough. Not only did she discover that Howard was an escaped convict—but she found that he was planning to rape and do away with her as soon as he could get her alone. A phone call to the local sheriff got Howard out of her life for good.

Another case turned out more favorably. Bruno P. had been asked by Milton C. to go into business with him. The deal sounded good, but Bruno was suspicious of Milton's motives. Probing Milton's mind with the Power Globe, he discovered that Milton really needed him and had no plans to cheat him. In fact, he was so impressed with Milton's honesty and ambition that he closed the deal the very next day. Within a few months, their new business was a tremendous success and they are now both earning in excess of $100,000 a year.

So, keep practicing. It won't take you long to get the hang of it, and after two or three encounters, you'll start to become more subtle. People will no longer be able to feel your mind probe—yet you'll be able to go deeper and deeper into their minds.

### Stage Two—How to Read Thoughts at a Distance

When you have thoroughly mastered Stage One, and are satisfied with your control of the Power Globe, you are ready for Stage Two, reading thoughts at a distance.

Once again, lie down in a quiet room and close your eyes. Expand the Power Globe to room size—and *keep expanding it*. Imagine it is the size of the building you're in—then the size of your block—then the size of your entire town. Keep going. Now the Globe is the size of your county. Now it is the size of your state. Now it is as big as the whole United States. Now it is the same size as the whole planet. STOP HERE. You have achieved Stage Two.

Practice Stage Two until you have it under full control. You will know when you have achieved this when the Power Globe around the Earth is as bright and strong in your mind as it was when it was room size.

Now try long-distance Ultra-Telepathy. Phone a friend as far away as possible, and try to read his or her mind. It is helpful if the friend is someone whose mind you have already read at close range. Use the same technique that you used to master Stage One, and keep trying with different people until you have achieved the results you want.

A young student, Kenneth A., used this method to keep tabs on his girl Hazel, while she was away at college. He phoned her every Sunday night, and not only found out what she was doing, but a whole lot more. After a few months, he drove out to the college, checked out the facts and shortly thereafter got himself a new girlfriend.

Another variation of this technique is to try it on people appearing on radio or TV. However, results are sometimes hard to achieve here because the soundtrack does not always represent what the people actually said, but is sometimes dubbed in later. Also, people are often reading scripts written by others, and thus it is hard to separate their own thoughts from those of the scriptwriter.

Still, you can have a very amusing time this way trying to read the thoughts of people who are being broadcast "live"—for example, those testifying at a Congressional hearing.

Stage Two is particularly effective when loved ones are involved. A case that comes to mind is that of Oscar T., an infantryman in Viet Nam. At the very instant he was wounded, his mother—over 6,000 miles away—felt a sharp, biting pain in the same leg he was wounded in. What made it even more remarkable was that his mother—even though she had mastered long-distance Ultra-Telepathy—was not consciously using it at the time!

More recently, Ruth L., a stenographer who had been looking for a husband for many years, found one as soon as she mastered Stage Two. Her problem was simply that she was very tall, and just couldn't seem to meet someone her height that she liked. A simple "psychonic broadcast" attracted men to her from all over the country—and for the first time in her life, she could actually take her pick of boyfriends. She soon married a wealthy doctor, and is now living happily in a luxury suburb of Los Angeles.

### Stage Three—The Impenetrable Mind Shield

Telepathy—ordinary telepathy, that is—has been around a long time. In fact, some interpretations of ancient Egyptian papyri have led modern Ultra-Psychonic scientists to believe that telepathy may have been in use as long ago as 4000 B.C.

Many people today know a smattering of these techniques, and often use them to their advantage against others. Perhaps you've been disturbed to find out that other people seem to know some of your most closely guarded secrets. It may well be that someone has picked them right out of your mind!

Obviously, you need protection against this sort of thing. That is why Stage Three of Ultra-Telepathy was developed. It consists of a mind-shield so solid, so massive that no one and nothing can ever get through it, including Ultra-Telepathy itself!

### How to Tell if Someone Is Reading Your Mind

How can you tell if someone is reading your mind? It's quite easy. If, for no reason at all, you find yourself thinking about your personal secrets—the intimate parts of your love life, for example, or how much money you have in the bank, or an embarrassing incident you never told anyone about—it may well be that someone is trying to read your mind by telepathic means.

There are two ways you can be sure. First of all, you will find that you're dwelling on parts of your secret that you already know—almost as if someone was asking question after question. "What bank is the money in?", for example, or "What's my lover's address?", or other obvious things you'd normally never think about.

The second proof is a bit more indirect. If, suddenly, people who you barely know start talking about your secrets—if people seem to have information about you that you never revealed—be suspicious. If, for instance, you're talking to someone about buying a new car and they say something like, "Oh, that's probably too much money for you," start to wonder.

Luckily, such probing and prying is easily stopped. What's more, there's a way to turn the tables on such snoopers and give them a lesson they'll never forget.

### SETTING UP THE ULTRA-TELEPATHIC MIND SHIELD

Lie down in a quiet room and set up a Stage One Power Globe, as you have learned. Expand it slowly to a Stage Two, pumping as much brightness and energy into it as you can.

Now, bring it slowly back down. Try to think of it as a giant balloon with a slow air leak. First, it is planet-size. Then, continent-size. Then, nation-size . . . state-size . . . county-size . . . town-size . . . building-size . . . room-size . . . Now, you're back down to Stage One—but you have 10,000 times as much power packed into it.

Keep shrinking the Power Globe. Now it's 5 feet in diameter . . . 3 feet . . . 2 feet . . . 1 foot. Stop it just inside your head. Then, using the enormous extra power you've just generated, visualize a metal shield completely surrounding the ball of light and energy.

Slowly, start to leak energy from the Power Globe into the shield. Keep adding more and more, until it seems to be glowing, getting "hotter" and "hotter," finally reaching a "white heat." (It is not physically hot, only telepathically—so there's no danger of it causing you any pain.)

Strangely enough, there really is a metallic shield around most of your brain. The bones of your skull contain calcium, which is a metal. Look it up in the periodic table of the elements, and you will find it in the same atomic group as beryllium and magnesium. It is also in the same group as radium, although it is not radioactive.

This is one of the great discoveries of Ultra-Telepathy—perhaps one of the most significant discoveries of the Twentieth Century—the discovery that the calcium in your bones *can be charged with telepathic energy!* It is one of the fundamental principles of Ultra-Psychonics.

Of course, your brain is not entirely shielded by bone. But when sufficient energy is put into the Mind Shield, there is about a 30% overlap—more than enough to seal off all the openings into the skull.

### Using the Mind Shield

Practice setting up the Mind Shield over and over, until you can do it in just a few seconds. Then watch what happens next time someone tries to "snoop" inside your mind!

Gregory M., a young executive, found his advancement completely stymied. No matter what clever idea he came up with, his rival, Max S., always seemed to get to the boss with it first. Yet Max never seemed to do much figuring or planning—and some of the ideas he came up with were based on things that only Gregory knew about.

Finally, Gregory heard about Ultra-Telepathy at a lecture he accidentally wandered into on his vacation. Before he returned, he mastered the Mind Shield technique—and turned it on the instant he set foot in the office.

To everyone's surprise, Max S. suddenly developed a "splitting headache" and went home at 9:30 that very morning. He seemed to get these headaches more and more frequently, and finally had to quit working altogether.

Meanwhile, Gregory rose like a rocket through the executive ranks, and became a full vice-president before the year was out.

That's how it works. Once you set up your Mind Shield, anyone trying to pry into your secrets will find that they've hit a white-hot wall. It's actually physically painful for them to keep trying, and no matter how hard they do so, all they get is a king-size headache for their trouble.

## Beyond Stage Three—The Mind Through Space and Time

Stages One, Two and Three of Ultra-Telepathy are more than enough for any normal use you might care to put it to. But if you're adventurous, and want to experiment, there are additional stages of development.

A word of apology: these advanced stages do not work for everyone. If you are really sincere, and put a great deal of time and effort into it, you have an 80% chance of success. But don't feel badly if you can't make it work, as your failure may be due to outside forces beyond your control.

For example, you may be trying to break through the wall of Time and contact one of your future descendants (Stage Five). But it is entirely possible that your great grandchildren do not have any children, and your line has ended with them.

At any rate, here are the more advanced stages of Ultra-Telepathy and some techniques you might want to try to attain them.

## Stage Four—Ultra-Telepathy with Animals

This works best with family pets, although theoretically you can use it on any creature with a brain. It will work on dogs, cats, birds, horses and some small rodents such as squirrels, gerbils and chipmunks. Don't waste your time trying it on turtles, goldfish or snakes—they just do not respond to Ultra-Telepathy for some reason.

Stage Four is a modification of Stage One. After you have

achieved a room-size Power Globe, take your family pet with you into a quiet room and stare at it steadily, willing it to come to you. As soon as it does so, reward it with a piece of food. Do this over and over, for a period of several days, until a human-animal telepathic channel is set up permanently. Now try to "feel" the animal's emotions—you will be astonished at the powerful blast of thought that comes through. You will feel love, hate, boredom, hunger, sex drive and a host of other emotions. Do not try to pick up human-type thoughts—animal minds simply don't work that way.

You can get many hours of enjoyment this way, especially if you and your pet are very close. You can find out what it wants, what it likes and dislikes and what it's afraid of. A useful side-benefit of this is that you can spot your pet's ailments before they develop into something really serious, and save yourself considerable time, worry and money.

Simon W., for example, recently saved close to $100 in vet fees when he discovered his cocker spaniel's limp was due entirely to jealousy of a new kitten his wife had brought home. The vet, unable to find any physical cause for the limp, had proposed exploratory surgery—and Simon had been all set for it. But when, through Stage Four communication, he discovered what the real problem was, he solved it right at home. A little extra affection, and the dog's limp disappeared almost overnight.

### Stage Five—Ultra-Telepathy Through Time

Have you ever wished you could sit down with some of the famous men and women of the past and talk to them, ask them intimate questions, get their advice or simply drink in their wisdom?

Have you ever wondered, for instance, exactly what happened between Mark Antony and Cleopatra? Or suppose you could sit down with a self-made millionaire like Henry Ford or John D. Rockefeller, and find out exactly how they got so rich? Is this possible?

It is, with Stage Five Ultra-Telepathy. Here's how to do it:

1. An hour before bedtime, sit down with a book by or about the famous person you want to "visit." Try to absorb the flavor of his time—the kind of clothes people wore then, what they ate, how they talked, what their main concerns were. It's helpful to know a little about their language if they didn't speak English,

although not entirely essential, since Ultra-Telepathy breaks through all language barriers. Still, each language generates its own kinds of thought patterns, and a little preparation can make things easier for you.

2. Just before you go to sleep, generate a Phase Two Power Globe and hold it firmly in your mind as you doze off. Concentrate on the person you are trying to reach—your subconscious mind will take care of the trip through time.

Noted scientists such as Dunne and Carrington have conducted experiments which seem to prove that the sleeping mind is free to move back and forth along the time track at will—and usually does.

How is this possible? As you have seen in previous chapters, Anti-Ultrons flow backwards through time. It is my belief that during the sleep process, the human brain generates both Ultrons and Anti-Ultrons unconsciously. Thus, the mind can "tune in" on either the past or future as it chooses, since it can flash along Ultron Beams into the past, or Anti-Ultron Beams into the future. And, since the whole operation takes places at the speed of thought, it's instantaneous!

It may even be possible that, under certain conditions of stress or during certain types of atmospheric disturbances (for example, violent storms or earthquakes), the mind may generate Ultrons and Anti-Ultrons spontaneously, in an attempt to defend itself.

This would tend to explain such phenomena as a drowning person seeing his entire life flash before his eyes, and the *"déjà vu"* effect. The latter effect has happened to almost everyone—it's that eerie feeling you get when something new seems to have happened to you before, or you go to a new place and it all looks familiar to you. If you've ever been in a strange place—and had the feeling that you've been there before—you've already experienced the proof of this.

3. Keep a pad and pencil next to the bed, and write down as much as you can remember as soon as you wake up. This is very important, because all of the details of your trip through time will vanish in a few minutes after you arise.

This same technique can be used to contact departed friends and relatives, although here the sensitizing instrument should be a photo or a letter from the deceased.

Trips into the future are taken in a similar fashion, although here the sensitizing problem becomes much more difficult. The easiest person to contact in the future is—yourself! Concentrate on reaching yourself at various future times in the future, and write down the results. This technique was used with great success by the noted scientist Dunne in his book, *An Experiment with Time.*

You can also try to contact future descendants of yours, future leaders of mankind and many others. The important thing is to work out a way to "sensitize" your mind before you go to sleep.

Is it possible to contact "fictional" characters such as Robin Hood, Tom Sawyer or James Bond? Some would say no. Yet other scientists have speculated on the existence of Alternate Worlds— worlds similar to ours, but separated by another dimension. They might be as close as the pages in a book, yet impossible to reach except through a method like Stage Five Ultra-Telepathy. In some of these worlds, there might really *be* a Robin Hood, Tom Sawyer or James Bond—and if so, you *might* be able to reach them. It's theoretically possible!

Can *you* do it? Try it and see.

A word of warning if you go into the future. NEVER, under any conditions, try to find out the date of your death. It will turn the rest of your life to ashes, because you'll always be waiting.

### Stage Six—Minds Across the Galaxies

For thousands of years, man has speculated whether or not there is life on other planets. In recent years, many of the world's top biologists have gradually come to the conclusion that there not only might be life elsewhere, but that there MUST BE.

A recent newspaper article speculated that there might be as many as 10,000 inhabited planets in our galaxy alone. Yet Government searches by giant radio telescopes such as were used a few years ago in Project Ozma have failed to turn up any signals from these other worlds.

Why haven't we heard from them?

One possibility might be that the beings on these worlds do not use radio at all. It is entirely possible that these creatures have perfected development of their minds over the centuries, and communicate entirely by telepathy!

If this is the case, it should be possible to get in touch with these beings by Ultra-Telepathy. A technique has been developed that seems to work, in some cases. I say *seems to work* because, obviously, there is no way of checking out the results.

Here is the step-by-step procedure to follow:

1. Establish a Phase One Power Globe and expand it to a Phase Two Power Globe around the planet, as usual.

2. Then, slowly but steadily, expand the globe of golden light out past the Earth's atmosphere. Now take it out past the Moon. Past Mars. Past Jupiter. Past Saturn, with its beautiful rings. Keep going. Finally, your Power Globe is the size of the entire Solar System. Stop there.

3. The Solar Power Globe will be quite weak, at first. But keep setting it up, day after day, for a week or two. You'll find by then that your mental telepathic "muscles" have developed beyond your wildest dreams. You now have as much psychic energy in the Solar Globe as you had in the Stage Two Globe. Contract this Globe down to Stage One room size—and you can almost *feel* the surging energies. And that's just the beginning.

4. In the next step, you will expand the Power Globe out beyond the limits of the Solar System and englobe the entire Galaxy. This will take quite a bit out of you at first, and I suggest you build yourself up physically somewhat with a diet of organically grown dried fruits and natural vitamins, in addition to your normal diet. Soon, however, you will be able to set up the Galactic Globe with ease.

5. Now comes the hardest part. Try to visualize the boundaries of the entire Universe. Think of it as a giant soap bubble—with every atom of soap an entire Galaxy. Expand your Power Globe around the bubble—and you have reached Stage Six—the Ultimate Power Globe!

6. After you have practiced Stage Six for a while, and have it under full control, start to search within it. "Listen" mentally for words, pictures, symbols, noises—anything that seems strange and different to you. Some experimenters have reported receiving such signals—and even more!

One man reported that, as his Globe swept across the planet Jupiter, he heard a series of high-pitched screams lasting for five or six seconds. Others have reported visions of great crowds of bird-like creatures frozen immobile, with their wings pressed against their ears to shut out some horrible, enormous sound. (Can some beings actually *feel* the Power Globe?)

Other researchers claim to have received more practical

messages from Out There. One man claims he was cured of a painful, lingering ailment by advice from outer space medicine men. Another claims to have gotten an idea for an invention that's already brought in $40,000. Did these ideas come from faraway planets? No one really knows.

## WHAT ULTRA–TELEPATHY CAN DO FOR YOU

You can readily see how superior Ultra-Telepathy is to the ordinary kind. But you really appreciate it when you put it to work for you:

- Use it to discover the secret thoughts of others—find out which stock is going to rise, which horse is going to win, which promotion is coming up.

- Use it to ward off psychic attacks—prevent others from "picking your brains," discover who your true friends really are, end spiteful talk behind your back, put a scare into your enemies.

- Use it to contact faraway friends—receive messages from others thousands of miles away, locate long-lost relatives, find out immediately about family emergencies.

- Use it to reach into the past—get guidance from the greatest men and women who ever lived, discover the location of buried treasures and lost mines, find out what really happened in history.

- Use it to see ahead through the years to come—learn the fate of your descendants, get advance news of new discoveries, cures and inventions, get warnings of disasters to avoid.

- Use it to "talk" to your pets—find out how much they really care for you, discover possible health problems, make them come to you by silent command.

- Use it to reach out to the stars—send your mind into the furthest reaches of the galaxies, see amazing sights no man has ever seen before, talk with super-intelligent beings who can help you.

- Use it to build a better life for yourself—a life filled to the brim with love, happiness, money, success, power and true peace of mind.

Remember, as you do these things, that you are not performing any kind of mysterious psychic feat or spiritual hocus-pocus. Your mind is using the laws of Ultra-Psychonics, just as your stomach uses the laws of Chemistry, and your legs use the law of Gravity.

Right now, as you are reading these words, your mind is emitting psychons, ultrons and egons in every direction. In order to put them to work for you, you must learn to control, focus and direct them. Just as a child learns to walk by mastering the law of Gravity, you, too, can learn to use Ultra-Telepathy through practice and application of the techniques set forth in this chapter.

# 13

## ULTRA-KINETICS:
## How to
## Manipulate Objects
## with Your Mind

---

Imagine, if you will, a scene in the desert. The time: 3,200 years ago. The blazing sun pours down on long lines of half-naked people yoked like cattle to giant blocks of stone. The pyramid of the great Pharaoh Khufu is being built. Inch by inch, foot by foot, mile by mile, great stone blocks weighing 2½ tons each are being dragged across the entire land of Egypt to build a tomb for the king.

At least, that's the way they show it in the movies. But there are those today who do not believe it. They point out that just one pyramid alone required 2,300,000 of those giant blocks, and they say that in those days there just weren't enough people to do it.

Figure it out for yourself. If, as the historians claim, it took 20 years to build the pyramid, that means over 115,000 blocks a year had to be moved . . . about 310 blocks a day. The truth is, it would be hard to move that many blocks today, even with machinery and heavy trucks. And there was more to it than just moving the blocks: giant ramps would have had to be built, camps and kitchens maintained, and everything else needed to support the multitudes of workers.

Is there another way the pyramids could have been built? "Yes," say some modern scholars, "by means of psycho-kinesis—the mental power that can move objects without touching them." And they may well be right. Surely it is no harder to imagine a small group of trained Egyptian priests moving such blocks by the force of their minds than it is to imagine every man, woman and baby in the kingdom working every day and night, 365 days a year, for 20 years.

If there were no other evidence for such psychic powers, of course, the conventional explanation would have to be believed. But today, with psychic research going on at a stepped-up pace all over the world, evidence is flooding in that psycho-kinesis is not only possible, but may well be a talent that every human being possesses.

I, myself, have seen uncut, unedited movies of the amazing Russian psychic, Mrs. Nelya Mikhailova, in which she moved pieces of bread and tableware around on a table purely by the force of her mind. It was one of the most astonishing sights I've ever seen, and if I had ever had any doubts about the reality of psycho-kinesis, they vanished then and there.

Magnetism? Hidden threads? Hardly. In other experiments, filmed before a panel of skeptical scientists, Mrs. Mikhailova separated the white of an egg from its yolk, while it was 6 feet away from her, floating in a tank of water; she moved cigarettes placed under a bell jar; made an entire wrist compass (plastic case, leather strap and all) spin like a carousel on a tabletop; and even made loose matches inside a clear plastic cube shuttle from side to side as if they were alive!

### The Secret of "Psychonic Tension"

Is Ultra-Psychonics involved in this phenomenon? I believe it is. Take, for example, the description of what happened when scientists measured the magnetic fields of Mrs. Mikhailova's body while she was actually using her psycho-kinetic powers: "The powerful magnetic fields around Mikhailova's body began to *pulse*! It was as if she'd caused a wave of energy to vibrate through the invisible energy-envelope around her. Not only was her entire force field pulsing, but the detectors showed that this pulsing force field had *focussed* in the direction of her gaze."

Note the similarities between this and the Ultronic and Psychonic Laser Beams you discovered in Chapter 1—right down to the focussing. And note the mysterious "wave of energy" that Mrs. Mikhailova emitted—a wave which Russian scientists could not identify. Could this be Ultra-Psychonic energy? I believe so.

Using this, and other, data, I have put together the elements of a new branch of Ultra-Psychonics . . . a branch I call "Ultra-Kinetics."

This new branch has one great virtue: it works. And what is more, its principles seem to explain many puzzling phenomena in the psycho-kinetic field such as poltergeist powers, levitation, astral travel and even possession.

The key to Ultra-Kinetics is a state I call "Psychonic Tension." Just as a famous exercise system develops the muscles of the body by pitting one muscle against the other, Psychonic Tension develops the lifting and moving "muscles" of the mind by pitting one mental power against another.

## How to Create a New Kind of Power Globe

In the last chapter, you learned how to create an Ultra-Telepathic Power Globe, using a beam of psychons.

In the same way, construct a beam of ultrons, using the cyclotron technique you learned in Chapter 1, and build it up into an expanding sphere of red light.

Holding the red sphere around your head at a distance of about 2 feet, expand a yellow Ultra-Telepathic Power Globe.

Now, holding the red ultronic Power Globe rigid with one part of your mind, try to force the yellow psychonic Power Globe *through* it. As you feel one or the other spheres start to "give," pour more power into it. To help yourself concentrate, clasp your hands together with your fingers interlocked in front of your chest. This is the "Psychonic Tension" ritual that develops your Ultra-Kinetic powers. Perform it for five minutes at a time, several times a day.

As your "Psychonic Tension" rituals continue, you will gradually notice a feeling of mental strength and well-being developing, even though you had felt perfectly fine before. Just as an athlete achieves a higher level of health while he is in training, so will you develop a higher level of psycho-atomic energy as your Ultra-Kinetic training continues.

After two weeks of the Psychonic Tension ritual, you will

feel the red Ultronic Power Globe literally crackling with energy whenever you set it up. You are now ready for your first Ultra-Kinetic matter manipulation.

## Control of Light

The easiest way to get started is by trying to control the smallest particle of matter that is available to you—the electron.

"But," you say, "I can't even see an electron." On the contrary, you not only can see them, you're seeing *by* them. If you're reading this book by electric light, for example, your light is coming from a metal wire inside the light bulb that is being heated by a stream of electrons passing through it.

In other words, if you can control the flow of electrons, you can control electricity.

To get the "feel" of the electron flow, practice turning a lamp off and on. Try to sense the surge of electrons when the light comes on, and the sudden cutoff when the light starts to go off.

Next, listen to a radio closely and try to get the "feel" of the way its power surges. Try controlling the sound volume with your mind. See if you can use your red Power Globe to interfere a little with the flow of electrons to the loudspeaker. Listen for slight variations in the sound—this means you are starting to control the flow.

Then practice on your TV set. See if you can delay the screen from lighting up for a few seconds after you turn it on. This will not hurt your TV set, but will help you increase your control.

Keep trying these techniques over and over, until you start to get definite, positive results. As you do so, you will feel your red Power Globe getting even stronger and more powerful.

In a very short time, you should have full control of this power.

## How Bruce O. Gets to Places Faster Through
## Control of Traffic Signals

One practical application of this technique is shortening the wait at traffic signals. Next time you're standing on a corner waiting for the light to change, try using your Power Globe to shut off the electricity to the red light and increase the flow to the green light. You'll be astonished at the results!

A relative of mine, Bruce O., has tried this with what he

reports are excellent results. A cab driver, he estimates that he saves at least an hour a day waiting for lights by using this method. Not only does he get to his destinations faster (usually getting a much better tip), but he says he also saves quite a bit of gas this way.

## Control of Chemical Reactions

The next step in developing your Ultra-Kinetic power is to extend it to the atomic and molecular level. Atoms and molecules are much larger than electrons, but they are still tiny enough to be easy to handle.

Take a small bottle, fill it with water and put in a pinch or two of black pepper. Then put on the cover and shake it up. Set it down on a table in front of you, and concentrate on slowing down the falling particles of pepper as they settle to the bottom of the bottle. Imagine that your red Power Globe has broken up into many, many little Power Globes, and each one is wrapped around a molecule of water. As the bits of pepper sink, bombard them from below with the water molecules under your control. You will notice that some bits of pepper are starting to sink more slowly than the rest.

You can also try similar experiments involving slowing down the rate at which sugar will dissolve in a cup of coffee, and slowing down the time it takes a pot of water to come to a boil.

Actually, once you master this method, you can use it to control any chemical reaction that you want to.

## How Eleanor J. Became a Master Chef

A young housewife I know has tried this chemical reaction control with great success. Her husband had been complaining about her cooking, and no matter how many cook books she read, she just couldn't seem to make things come out any better.

However, once she started to use Ultra-Kinetics, she said that things definitely started to improve. She discovered she could mentally "taste" each dish as she finished each step in its preparation, and found that it became much simpler to correct the flavor then, before the dish was hopelessly ruined.

## Control of Small Objects

The next step for more Ultra-Kinetic power is to try moving

small objects. Start out with a feather. Drop it to the floor in front of you, and as it slowly falls, try to mentally "nudge" it with your red Power Globe so that it falls where you want.

Then, try rolling marbles or small ball bearings across the floor, and concentrate your Ultra-Kinetic powers on changing their direction. Gradually, work up to tennis balls and larger objects.

### How Elmer W. Controls the Fall of Dice

Can it be done? Elmer W. thinks so. He overheard me talking about Ultra-Kinetics to a member of my bowling team a few weeks ago, and seems to have applied it to his gambling activities. I haven't seen him since, but the grapevine reports that Elmer is making a fortune shooting dice these days.

"Watch out for Elmer," warned my informant. "He just can't lose."

### Control of Larger Objects

How large an object can you move? It's hard to say. The general principle seems to be that if you can lift an object physically, you can lift it mentally. Thus, you should be able to move a chair or a table after you develop your full powers, but it's unlikely you could move something very heavy like a safe or a refrigerator (unless you can move them now, of course). Still, there are some cases on record which seem to indicate that these limits can be exceeded in emergencies.

### How Jason W. Saved His Brother's Life
### in an Auto Accident

One such case is that of Jason W., who said that he had a dream in which his younger brother's car skidded off the road and turned over, with his brother caught underneath.

Jason was frantic. In his dream, he reached out with hysteric strength and lifted the car off his brother. At this point, he awoke in a cold sweat and tried to phone his brother. No one was home.

The next day, he heard that his brother was in the hospital, and went to visit him. His brother had no recollection of what had happened, except that he had crashed and was in terrible pain because his legs were under the car. Suddenly the pain eased up, and he fainted.

The motorist who found him said that he was at least a dozen feet from the car when he arrived. "I don't know how he could've gotten there with two broken legs," he said.

## The Ultronic Poltergeist Technique

Poltergeists have been around for many centuries. They make objects fly around the room, chandeliers swing violently to and fro, people trip and fall for no apparent reason and do many other strange things.

It has only been in recent years, however, that occult researchers have been able to trace the causes of such manifestations. They have usually turned out to be caused by a frustrated or unhappy teenage child, whose psychic powers somehow become enormously magnified to "revenge" herself on her relatives. Exorcism rites are usually useless in such cases, but calming the child down and resolving her frustrations often puts an end to them.

However, anyone can produce such manifestations with the help of Ultra-Kinetics, it turns out, since what happens in such cases is simply a violent, rapid movement of a fully energized Ultronic Power Globe around a room.

"Why would anyone want to do such a thing if they're not a frustrated teenager?" you ask.

Well, there might be many reasons. Perhaps you might want to frighten away a burglar you hear prowling around downstairs ... perhaps you might want to alert your neighbors to an emergency during which you are unable to move ... or perhaps you want to give someone a really convincing demonstration of your psychic powers.

## How to Make Objects Fly

The technique itself is fairly simple, provided you have achieved sufficient control of your Ultra-Kinetic powers. Here's how to do it:

1. Create your strongest possible Ultronic Power Globe, about 2 feet in diameter.

2. Now, imagine that it is rising up above your head like a balloon rising up on a long "string" of the same kind of red ultronic energy.

3. Next, start to twirl the "string" around your head, faster

and faster, until the ball of energy on the end is swinging around your head horizontally. Concentrate on its being hard and heavy.

4. Finally, pick your target, and send the ball crashing into it, again and again.

5. After you have demolished this object, retrieve the ball, and start it swinging again. Lengthen the "string" it is swinging on until it is long enough to reach the next object you want to hit, and let it fly again.

6. When you are all finished, carefully reel in the Power Globe until it surrounds your head once more. Then soften it up and collapse it very carefully until it is all gone. This is very important, since you may get a splitting headache if you don't turn it off correctly.

## How Sophie C. Got Her In-Laws to Stop Bothering Her

A young newlywed I know recently used the Ultronic Poltergeist technique to great effect in getting her married life off on the right foot.

Sophie C. was afflicted with snoopy, bossy in-laws, who were driving her right up the wall. She was delighted with the Ultronic Poltergeist technique when I described it to her, and put it to work a few weeks later.

The next time her relatives came barging in the door, things started to happen. Her mother-in-law tripped on the rug and almost broke her neck. Her father-in-law's cigarette lighter flared up and singed his mustache. And her obnoxious little brother-in-law found himself mysteriously locked in a closet he was prowling around in, and couldn't get out for hours.

It got even better the next time. This time, she visited them—and things really popped. Pictures flew off the wall. The dinner burned up right in the oven. And the dishwasher went berserk, and smashed up all the chinaware.

Her in-laws don't know what her powers are, but she says they're a lot nicer and more polite to her these days—when they even dare show up.

## The Secret of Personal Ultra-Levitation

If you can make objects fly, what about yourself? Yes, it's

really possible, and such feats of levitation have been witnessed and written up for centuries.

In Tibet, for example, the famous *lung-gom-pa* adepts, were said to be able to generate a force that apparently counteracts gravitation. A noted French scientist who met one reported that one such adept "seemed to lift himself from the ground." These adepts are reputed to be able to "sit on an ear of barley without bending its stalk."

In more modern times, the noted psychic Olof Jonsson has not only been able to levitate himself in public, but has even been photographed doing so.

The Ultra-Levitation technique for doing this is not too difficult, but takes quite a bit of practice. Here's what to do:

1. Remove all your clothes and stand on a bathroom scale.

2. Generate the Ultronic Power-Globe on a "string" as you did for the Ultronic Poltergeist technique.

3. This time, instead of letting it swing, concentrate on making it rise like a balloon, lifting you with it.

4. Keep your eyes on the dial of the scale. It will start to drop, bit by bit, showing that you are getting lighter.

Do not expect complete success at first, but repeated attempts will gradually get you the results you desire.

### How Victor T. Was Saved from Drowning

Victor T., an elderly neighbor of mine, credits this technique with saving his life. He's never really been able to make it work fully for him, as he's always been a bit of a skeptic about occult phenomena, but he has been trying it off and on.

Last summer, his boat overturned and he fell into the water fully clothed. As the weight of his wet clothing started to drag him down, he made a mighty mental effort and generated a rising Power Globe. To his surprise, he rose back out of the water, and was able to stay with his head above the surface for almost 10 minutes, until another neighbor sailed up and rescued him.

"I should have been wearing a life jacket," Vic admits, "but thank the Lord, I had something better."

Admittedly, there are not too many practical applications for Ultra-Levitation—but this is certainly one of them!

## The Secret of Psychonic Invisibility

How would you like to be invisible? To walk through the streets of a city unseen and unnoticed? To enter any building, mingle with any group and be completely unobserved?

Impossible? Perhaps. I remember once in Ravenna, a few years ago, I attempted to take a photo of a strange-looking man who didn't like the idea. He pointed his finger at my camera, gave me a peculiar, penetrating look—and the film came out blank. The regent of Tibet, Gyalpo, also possessed this power. In the 1930's, a European professional camera crew filmed him in both color and black-and-white, as part of a documentary they were making. Hundreds of photos were taken—yet only one came out, and that one was one in which the regent was making fun of the camera crew!

Fogging the film in a camera is easy, of course, especially with a variation of the Ultronic Poltergeist technique. Just generate a small Power Globe about the size of an orange, and send it crashing through the camera lens. The photographer will get a big surprise when he develops the film!

However, in order to achieve full Psychonic Invisibility, the spirit must leave the body and travel along the Astral Pathways. Here is how to do it:

1. Lie down in a darkened room, and make yourself as comfortable as possible. This is important, as otherwise you may get severe muscle cramps when you return to your body.

2. Generate the red Ultronic Power Globe, and let it rise like a balloon above your head, on its psychic "string."

3. Imagine that your spirit—your ego—in short, *you*—are flowing through a hollow tube in the center of the "string" into the center of the Power Globe.

4. Now imagine that the "string" is getting longer and longer. The Power Globe will float up through the roof, and out over the town.

5. Direct the Power Globe to go wherever you want to be. No one can see it, or you—yet you can penetrate everywhere: through walls, beyond locked doors, into the most intimate recesses of people's lives.

6. Do not stay out too long. It is dangerous to be away from your body more than two hours at most.

7. To return, reverse the process. Shorten the string, bit by bit, until you are back in the room where you started.

8. Let your spirit flow back through the "string" into your body.

9. Then, and only then, reel in the Power Globe until it surrounds your head again, and slowly shrink it down to nothingness.

## How Veronica S. Turned the Tables on a Peeping Tom

Veronica S., a liberated young lady I know, was quite annoyed by a neighbor's kid who kept watching her with binoculars through her open shades.

"That little creep really bugs me," she confessed, "and his mother won't do a thing about it. She thinks it's funny."

Using Ultronic Astral Travel a few nights later, Veronica paid a special visit to her nosy little friend. To her delight, she spotted him taking money out of his mother's handbag while she was out.

A few words to the boy's mother, and he was sent away to a military school, where the only view from his window was a flagpole.

## A New Kind of Astral Travel

If you have done any research into the techniques used up until now to induce astral travel, you will recognize that the Ultronic method is quite new.

Although it uses some of the techniques developed and perfected over the ages, it has one unique feature which the others lack: it is entirely safe, provided the techniques spelled out above are followed step-by-step.

Unlike the other methods, your spirit is safe at all times, protected by the energized walls of the Ultronic Power Globe. No person or thing can get at you, nor can even the most sensitive psychic even become aware of your visitation.

## How Eric D. Escapes from His Wheelchair

Eric D., a middle-aged former musician, now crippled by

arthritis and confined to a wheelchair, has found Ultronic Astral Travel a true godsend. Once ready to commit suicide, he has found a new life.

With its help, he visits concerts and operas all over the world—sees the greatest singers and the finest orchestras—and even manages to "drop in" on his former friends and associates to see how they're getting along.

"At last, I have something to live for again," he says.

### Ultra-Puppetrics: How to Take Psychonic Possession of Other People's Bodies

For those who like to live dangerously, there is one final, and advanced technique of Ultra-Kinetics. It is a development of the Ultronic Astral Travel technique, and what it does is to let you take possession of other people's bodies to a certain extent.

That is, you can see out of their eyes, hear with their ears and experience their thoughts and emotions. You cannot make them do anything they would not normally want to do, nor can you communicate with them in any way. However, just "possessing" their bodies can be quite exciting if it is done at the proper time.

The technique consists of approaching the people you want to "possess" by Ultronic Astral Travel, hovering above them, and then dropping a psychic "string" down into their heads.

Your spirit then flows along the "string" and into their body. That's all there is to it. There is one element of danger, however. You must maintain the Power Globe, with both "strings" attached, at all times. If either one is forgotten about, and disappears, you may find that you're stuck in the other person's body—permanently.

## WHAT ULTRA-KINETICS CAN DO FOR YOU

In this chapter, you've seen:

- How the ancient wizards built colossal works of stone with their psychic powers.

- How "Psychonic Tension" can develop the kinetic powers of the mind by pitting the mind's inner forces against themselves.

- How to generate an Ultronic Power Globe.

- How to begin your control over matter with control on the electronic level.

- How to control chemical reactions on the atomic and molecular levels of the universe.

- How to manipulate small objects such as dice, roulette wheels and lottery tickets.

- How to move fairly large objects with your Ultra-Kinetic powers.
- How to produce the Ultronic Poltergeist effect and make ordinary objects fly around a room.

- How to counteract the force of gravity with Ultra-Levitation.

- How to make yourself impossible to photograph.

- How to become invisible and intangible with Ultronic Astral Travel.

- How to invade the minds and bodies of others with the technique of Ultra-Puppetrics and learn their innermost secrets.

... These secrets have been guarded ... and misunderstood for centuries by the great mystics and occult researchers. Now, for the first time, the truth is in your hands. Use it wisely.

# 14

## ULTRA-SOPHOLOGY:
### How to
### Find the Way to
### True Happiness

---

The power to read minds . . . the power to dominate others . . . the power to find hidden treasures . . . and
all of the others . . . are only means to an end.

No matter how much wealth, power and psychic
energy you possess, if you are not happy, you really
have nothing.

That is why the ultimate branch of Ultra-Psychonics deals with the pathway to true happiness and
peace of mind. Follow this pathway, and no matter
what else happens, you will experience the greatest
pleasure and joy that a human being can know. Ignore it,
and no matter what else you achieve, your life will be
empty and unfulfilled.

### The Ultra-Psychonic Secret of Lasting Happiness

Here, then, are the Ten Actions of Joy, which will
help you find the kind of life you've always wanted—a
life filled to the brim with gladness and delight. Each

action is psychonically charged, and as you perform these actions in your daily life, you will feel a sense of warmth and fulfillment within yourself:

ACTION #1–THE JOY OF GIVING

> This action involves helping those who are less fortunate than yourself, but it is not limited to them. You can also give things to those you love and care for. And you can give nonmaterial things, such as admiration, respect and sympathy. The more you give, the more you will receive.

ACTION #2–THE JOY OF HUMILITY

> This action involves acceptance of yourself for what you are, without pride or haughtiness. It means that you must treat everyone with equal respect and courtesy, regardless of how much you may be superior or inferior to them.

ACTION #3–THE JOY OF WORKING

> This action involves putting your full effort into everything you do, whether you do it for yourself or for another. It means not holding back, not slacking off, but giving your all at all times.

ACTION #4–THE JOY OF CARING

> This action involves reverence for life. It means that you must never kill or hurt any living thing. It means that you must *care* what happens to others, whomever they may be, and try to help them as much as you possibly can.

ACTION #5–THE JOY OF FIDELITY

> This action involves loyalty to those who love you and to your friends. It means that you must never betray their trust and never abandon them. It does not mean you must condone their wrongdoing, since this does not really help them.

ACTION #6–THE JOY OF SUFFICIENCY

> This action involves satisfaction and enjoyment of the things you have. A Hindu sage once said, "The secret of happiness is not in wanting more, but in desiring less." Cast out greed and envy from your mind, and take pleasure in what you have earned.

## ACTION #7–THE JOY OF CALMNESS

This action involves control of your passions and emotions. It means that you should control events, rather than letting events control you. You should avoid anger, jealousy, resentment and other negative emotional states.

## ACTION #8–THE JOY OF LEARNING

This action involves the improvement and development of your mind. Just as you improve and develop the furnishing and decoration of your home, so, too, should you fill your mind with useful knowledge and helpful information.

## ACTION #9–THE JOY OF MEDITATION

This action involves contemplation of yourself, others and the Universe on a regular basis. Set aside half an hour a day for this purpose, and you will soon note a tremendous difference in your outlook on life.

## ACTION #10–THE JOY OF REVERENCE

This action involves merging yourself into the Cosmic Mind, according to the principles of your faith, on a regular basis. It means that you submit yourself to a Higher Power, and by doing so, gain everything worth gaining.

### Why Ultra-Sophology Is Acceptable to All Religions

Ultra-Sophology is acceptable to all religious faiths because it is not a religion itself—merely a way of seeing the world in terms of the great Truths that all faiths preach.

### How Boris I. Achieved True Peace of Mind

One of the things I've done recently that gave me the greatest pleasure was to introduce Boris I. to the Ten Actions of Joy. Boris, the owner of a small local factory, was the nearest thing to Scrooge that could exist outside of a book. His factory, only marginally profitable, was constantly racked by battles with the union; and his executive staff turned over so fast that you'd think they were going through a revolving door as soon as he hired them.

After several long talks, one stretching into the wee hours of the morning, I finally convinced Boris that he ought to give the Ten Actions of Joy a try. It was quite a personal battle for him, because it was so different from the way he had been living and thinking up until that time.

The first noticeable effect was that the turnover of his top executives suddenly stopped. Gradually, he told me, a new atmosphere began to pervade his factory. The union began to get more friendly, and the workers' chip-on-the-shoulder attitudes started to fade away.

Now, for the first time in years, he recently confided, profits have taken a dramatic upsurge, despite increased costs due to the energy shortage. Instead of filing for bankruptcy, he's thinking of opening a second plant.

## How to Achieve Cosmic Illumination

Down through the ages, the greatest minds of mankind have sought the goal of Cosmic Illumination—the freeing of the human mind from the bondage of the material world, the Great Enlightenment.

Those who have achieved this advanced psychic state report that it is the most wonderful experience known to mankind. There are many ways to do it—some taking many years, some taking considerably less. Zen Buddhism, for example, is primarily concerned with this problem, and has worked out a series of meditations called "koans" (from the Chinese "kung-an") which can, reportedly, shorten the timespan enormously.

It is my belief that these "koans" are definitely connected with Ultra-Psychonics—that meditating upon the seemingly insoluble questions they raise somehow *charges* the psychons, ultrons and egons that make up the human mind's psychic atoms with a special kind of spiritual energy. When the charge reaches a certain level, I believe there is a "breakthrough" into a higher energy state—the state we call Cosmic Illumination or Enlightenment.

What is this state like? One person described it as "a sudden flood of light inside my soul, like sunrise after years in the dark. I knew the exact conditions of all living beings, throughout all the worlds and all the ages. I saw the Cause and Effect of all things."

There are many "koans," of increasing difficulty, and it is hard to say how many a particular person would have to go through until he achieves Cosmic Illumination. Some are reported to have reached the goal almost immediately, others have not.

It would take an entire book just to list the "koans" that are used today, and obviously I cannot do it here. But I will give you the first two:

1. What did your face look like before you were conceived?

2. What is the sound of one hand clapping?

Meditate on the solution to these two "koans" until you are certain that you know the answers. You will know that your answers are correct when other "koans" start to occur to you.

## The Master Plan of the Universe

In other parts of this book, you have seen how anti-particles prove the existence of an Anti-Universe co-existing with our own. Perhaps you have wondered whether there could be a map or a blueprint that would show how the entire Cosmos fits together.

The ancient Chinese pondered this question for many thousands of years, and eventually they came up with such a map . . . a Master Plan of the Universe.

Naturally, such a map cannot be literal . . . if it were, it would be the size of a mountain, or even larger; and not very useful, since it would be in a constant state of change. The wise men of the East eventually realized that such a map must be symbolic. Here is what it looks like:

Study this map carefully, for it is deceptively simple. It shows both the Universe and the Anti-Universe . . . and it shows that in each of them, there is an entry point into the other. This helps explain how you can manipulate the anti-particles of the Anti-Universe and use them in this one.

But the meaning of the map is much deeper than that. It tells you, for example, that every favorable situation contains a tiny seed of disaster in it; and that every unfavorable situation contains a tiny seed of salvation.

It tells you that even the best person is not perfectly good, nor the worst person perfectly bad. It tells you that your worst enemies can be turned into friends, if you are careful; and your best friends can become enemies, if you are not.

There is much, much more in this symbol. Include it in your meditations, and you will be amply rewarded.

## The Atomic Rites

One immediate application of this Cosmic Map, however, is in the field of prayer.

It points the way to a new kind of prayer—a scientifically based, logically structured method that, I believe, is much more effective than the usual, old-fashioned method. Not that many old-fashioned prayers do not work—it's a proven fact that they do. But it's always been sort of a hit-and-miss proposition.

The Atomic Rites, as I call them, do not substitute for your regular way of praying . . . they merely amplify it and clarify it with "powered thoughts."

In the next few sections of this chapter, you will discover some of these "powered thoughts" and see how you can use them to help you pray for riches, love, power, friendship, health and many other things, more productively.

## How Helga A. Overcame Her Sordid Past

Before we move on to the specific techniques, however, I think you'll be interested in hearing how this new type of prayer helped an unfortunate woman make a fresh start in life.

Helga A. was trapped into a life of crime at an early age. By the time she was 30, she had been arrested for everything from streetwalking to shoplifting. "Please help me," she begged.

I showed Helga the Master Plan of the Universe and explained its meaning to her. She was surprised to learn that deep within herself lay the key to her rescue. Bit by bit, she took the spot of respectability on the vast expanse of criminal activity, and began to expand it. Bit by bit, through prayer and the Atomic Rites, she received help to build a new life for herself. Finally, she became free of her past and is earning her living as a nurse in a hospital in the Midwest.

"Please tell people," she recently wrote, "how I was saved from the pits of Hell. Tell them that you may be down, but you're never out."

### The Ultra-Psychonic Ritual for Riches

What *are* the Atomic Rites? They are special words—call them chants or rituals, if you will—that are added to regular prayers to reinforce them. Just as an electric light outshines a candle, just as a loudspeaker amplifies your voice, these special Ultra-Psychonic rituals "boost" your prayers to a higher level of energy.

For example, if you are praying for riches, after you have finished whatever prayers are appropriate to your faith, you would add these words:

In wealth there is poverty, in poverty are the seeds of wealth. Help me to plant the seeds of wealth, to nourish them and make them grow.

Then, for the next five minutes, meditate on just two things:

1. What seeds of wealth lie within you right now?

2. How will you use this wealth to help others, as well as yourself?

After the five minutes are up, sit silently for a while and "listen" with your mind. Suddenly, it will become clear to you just what you must do—as if a Voice was speaking to you.

### How Marvin R. Was Lifted from Poverty

Can this Atomic Rite help you? If it could help Marvin R., I believe it can help anyone. Marvin R. was a penniless hobo who came to my door several years ago and asked for a handout.

I took him in, fed him and talked to him about Ultra-Sophology. "I don't believe it, but I'll try anything," he said, "I'm sick and tired of this rotten life."

I watched his face as he prayed and performed the Atomic Rite. It was perfectly blank, and then suddenly, like the sun rising, it was lit up from within.

"Thank you," he said, "I know what to do now." Then he left.

A few years later, I heard from a friend that Marvin R. had gone out to the West Coast, and opened up one of the most successful restaurants in the Los Angeles area. And I also heard that he is using much of the money he now earns to help rehabilitate other men and women who are temporarily "down on their luck."

## The Ultra-Psychonic Ritual for Love

Love, too, can be aided and supported with the Atomic Rites. The Ultra-Psychonic Ritual for love is similar to the one for riches—for love is the greatest treasure of all.

After you have finished whatever prayers are appropriate to your faith, add these words:

> From love came hate, but in hate are the seeds of love. Help me to plant the seeds of love, to nourish them and make the tree of affection bloom and blossom.

Then, for the next five minutes, meditate on just two things:

1. What is there in you that is worthy of being loved?
2. How will you return the love that you are so urgently seeking?

After the five minutes are up, sit silently and "listen" with your mind. Quietly, you will become aware of exactly what you must do to win the love of the person you care about.

## How Nancy P. Regained Her Husband's Affection

Nancy P. was in quite a predicament when I met her. She had run away from her husband and family to go off with a former boyfriend. In a few months, she was pregnant, and her boyfriend walked out on her.

"How could I be so stupid?" she sobbed. "How can I ever fix things up?" I told her exactly what to do.

As she performed the Atomic Rite for love, a change seemed to come over her. Her eyes grew softer, and for the first time since I had met her that evening, she smiled a little.

Then she picked up the phone and called her husband. A few hours later, she got on a bus and went back to her home town. She must have received powerful help from the Atomic Rite, for since then I have been receiving annual Christmas cards from her and her husband—and from the children, old and new.

## The Ultra-Psychonic Ritual for Power

Can power over others come from a prayer? Certainly, if the power is intended for worthwhile purposes. Church leaders, for instance, have such power, and so do heads of charitable institutions.

After you have finished whatever prayers are appropriate to your faith, add these words:

In strength there is weakness, but in weakness there is strength.
Help me to plant the seeds of strength, to nourish them and make them grow.

Then, for the next five minutes, meditate on just two things:
1. What resources of untapped power lie within you now?

2. How will you use your power over others to help them?

Shortly after the five minutes of meditation have finished, you will know exactly what you must do to gain the power over others that you are seeking. "Listen" for the answer.

## How Edward M. Became Mayor of His Town

Edward M. had been trying to become mayor of a nearby town for several years without much success, when I met him.

He almost choked on his lunch when I suggested the Atomic Rites to him. "I'd be the laughingstock of the county, if I did something like that," he snorted.

"You don't understand, Ed," I said. "It isn't something you do on a speaker's platform or at a political rally. It's something you do in the privacy of your home."

Ed never would tell me if he had tried the Atomic Rites. But in the next campaign, he was a new man. Instead of simply attacking the opposition, he spoke about what the town needed, and how he could help them get it. He put forth such excellent ideas, in fact, that his opponent even adopted some of them!

Needless to say, Ed won the election handily.

## The Ultra-Psychonic Ritual for Friendship

There are prayers that bring new friends, and others that

mend broken friendships. Both are strengthened with the help of the Atomic Rites.

After you have finished whatever prayers are appropriate to your faith, add these words:

> Friends can turn into strangers, but strangers can be turned into friends. Help me to plant the seeds of friendship, to nourish them and make them grow. And help me to keep the friends I have now, well and strong.

Then, for the next five minutes, meditate on just two things:

1. Why should others seek you out as a friend?

2. How will you help your present friends, and the new friends whom you soon will be meeting?

After you have meditated on these questions for five minutes, "listen" once more with your mind. As if a Voice has spoken, you will know what you must do to find new friends, and how to keep the friendships you now have.

## How Carol E. Found New Friends in a Hostile Community

A relative of mine, Carol E., recently wrote from the South that she has finally been accepted by the community.

It was not always so. When she moved there a few years ago, she found a great deal of hostility, simply because she was from another section of the country. It got so bad, in fact, that she was thinking of moving back.

But I persuaded Carol to try the Atomic Rite for friendship. She was astonished at the results. Within two weeks, she was invited to join one of the leading women's organizations in the area. People who had been ignoring her suddenly started to say "Good morning!" and smiled at her when they met. And the people who lived around her, who had been particularly unfriendly, suddenly turned into model neighbors.

"I can't understand it," she wrote me, "I am still the same person I always was, but something has changed."

## The Ultra-Psychonic Ritual for Health

Prayers for health are widely said. When all else fails, there is one Source that can help—a Power that has worked miracles of healing. Here is how to summon this help, with the Atomic Rites.

After you have finished whatever prayers are appropriate to your faith, add these words:

In health are the germs of sickness, in sickness are the seeds of health. Help me to plant the seeds that will destroy the germs to nourish my body and restore me again.

Then, for the next five minutes, meditate on just two things:

1. Do you feel that your illness is a punishment for something you may have done or failed to do?

2. How will you use your health, when it is restored to you?

After five minutes, when your meditation is finished, you will understand the true cause of your illness and you will feel the Healing Power starting to flood into you.

### How Dennis L. Overcame His Drinking Problem

There are those who say that alcoholism is a sickness, and not a vice. Dennis L. is one of them. For many years, he was controlled by a drinking problem that was growing increasingly worse. He lost his job, his family left him and finally he was thrown out on the street by his landlord. Then his health started to fail him.

Dennis had always been a fighter, but he just couldn't seem to come to grips with this adversary. "I just can't stop drinking," he told me, "even if it kills me."

But with the help of the Atomic Rites, he came to realize that he drank out of a feeling of guilt—guilt about neglect of his spiritual obligations. And with this realization, the seeds of health started to grow within him. Starting as a helper in a Skid Row mission, Dennis gradually regained his health as he worked to aid others, and as he began to participate again in the spiritual life he had repudiated for so many years.

Today, restored in body and soul, he is one of the leading figures in the church in his area. As the Bible says, "Ask, and it shall be given you."

### The Ultra-Psychonic Ritual for Golden Blessings

Finally, there is the Atomic Rite for those who neither need nor want any material thing, but simply want to receive the Golden Blessing that is the greatest of all gifts.

After you have finished whatever prayers are appropriate to your faith, add these words:

The light fades and there is darkness. But out of the darkness, comes the light again. Help me to plant the seeds of light, to nourish my spirit and to receive the radiance of the Golden Blessing.

Then, light a single candle in a darkened room, and look into it for five minutes while you meditate on just two things:

1. Do you feel you are worthy to receive the Golden Blessing?

2. If, despite any feelings of unworthiness you may have, you *do* receive the Golden Blessing, what will you do to become more worthy of it?

After the five minutes are up, you will feel an inner radiance starting to permeate your entire being. But it is only a tiny beginning—its growth will depend on how worthy you become to receive it.

## How Matt M. Was Forgiven by Those He Had Wronged

Matt M., a young college student I know, had brought considerable shame on his family. He was arrested for burglary, and seemed destined for a long stretch in the penitentiary.

But another friend of mine saw Matt before the trial, and talked to him about the Atomic Rites and the Golden Blessing. Matt was at the end of his rope—his family refused to help him, most of his former friends would have nothing to do with him and his girlfriend broke off their engagement. He felt he had nothing left, so he asked for nothing—only for the Golden Blessing.

Then things started to change for him. The court appointed a lawyer to defend him who was more than just a lawyer—a man who had a deep understanding of the ways of the mind. He talked to Matt and showed him how he had almost ruined his entire life. He talked to the people whose house Matt had burgled, and showed them what Matt's conviction would mean. And he talked to Matt's family, and brought them back to his side.

Matt was convicted, nevertheless. But he received a suspended sentence, and with his family and friends once more trying to help him, he turned his back on his past, and carved out a new life for himself as a youth counselor. He is extremely effective in his new position, he says, "perhaps because I have walked that road myself."

## Secrets of the Bardo Thodol

You have come a long way. You have probed the innermost secrets of the mind, discovered practical Ultra-Psychonic techniques to help you in your everyday life, found out how to develop and use amazing psychic powers and learned new ways to receive spiritual help and enrichment.

Is there anything more? Yes. There is the question of what lies beyond the gates of the Hereafter. You are, of course, already familiar with the traditional Western views on the subject, but there are others.

The Tibetans, for example, have a very unusual scripture called the *Bardo Thodol,* or *Book of the Dead.* It is not a ceremony of burial, but a set of instructions for the deceased—a guide through the mystic realm of the Bardo, a state of existence that lasts for 49 days after death, until the next reincarnation.

The Tibetans believe that at the moment of death, a supreme insight and illumination is granted. Soon afterwards, strange illusions begin, and the insight and illumination starts to fade away. Eventually, the visions become so terrifying that—unless the mind has been prepared for them—the mind starts to deteriorate and lapse back into a purely animalistic state of being. Such a mind begins to fall prey to sexual fantasies, and is lured by the vision of mating couples. The mind is thus easily "caught" by a womb and then reborn into the earthly world, there to go through the entire cycle again.

But the mind that is prepared—the mind that recognizes and holds onto its moment of supreme illumination—does not disintegrate. Instead, it moves to a higher plane of being and merges into the Immutable Light, the Cosmic Mind of the Universe.

"Very interesting," you say, "but how does this apply to me?"

It applies in one important way: If you are now afraid of death, it indicates that death may not be the end of everything, but merely a new beginning. It means that no matter how bad or how hopeless things look now, you will get a second chance.

## The Ultra-Psychonic Meaning
## of the Book of the Dead

Another ancient book, the *Egyptian Book of the Dead,* is quite different from the *Bardo Thodol.* Its Hereafter is a courtroom—a judgement scene in which the departed soul first must plead its innocence in a series of "Negative Confessions," and then must hand its heart over to be weighed on a scale, balanced against the Feather of Truth.

If the heart was pure, the deceased led a life of bliss and happiness from then on. If the scale fell the other way, the heart was devoured by a crocodile.

"A pretty fable," you say, "but, again, how does it apply?"

It is interesting, of course, only in an historical sense. But it indicates that for many thousands of years, long before any of the present-world religious systems came into existence, mankind believed that there would be judgement for its actions after death. This was hardly an obvious belief—actually, it would be more to people's advantage to believe the opposite. It must have been based on something *real*—on psychic and mystical experiences that the ancient papyrus scrolls can only hint at.

What it means to you is this: your powers—Ultra-Psychonic and otherwise—should be used only for worthwhile purposes. If you use them for evil, not only is there the danger that they will "backfire" upon you while you are alive, but they may provide a very unpleasant experience for you afterwards.

### The Meaning of Life

All of the foregoing adds up to one thing: you have been placed upon this Earth for a *purpose*. A cosmic mission has been assigned to you, and you must discover what it is.

If you find your mission in life, and fulfill it, you will be rewarded in many ways. If you do not find it, or fail to fulfill it, you will be punished. It's as simple as that.

The choice is up to you.

### How to Find Your Place in the Book of Destiny

As you learned earlier, Destiny is not fixed but fan-shaped. There are innumerable paths open before you, dependent on your free will. Yet, in order to fulfill your true purpose in life, you must choose the correct path.

How can you do this?

One way is through meditation. Each morning, after you wake up, but before you get out of bed, meditate on these two questions:

1. What am I capable of accomplishing today?

2. Which of these things will help me most to fulfill my cosmic mission?

After a few minutes, when you have finished meditating, the correct answers will come to you. Fix them firmly in your mind, and act accordingly.

### How Roy D. Was Saved from Suicide and Found His True Purpose in Life

The best illustration of this lies in the life of Roy D., who owes his life to it. Roy, an elderly man living on the income from his investments, suddenly found that he had been "wiped out" in the stock market. He began to seriously think about ending it all.

I talked him out of it with just one question, "Is making money in the stock market your real purpose in living?"

Roy was shocked. He had never thought about things that way. He began to realize that money was only the means to an end. He saw that he still had the things that really counted—his family, his friends, the respect of his neighbors.

Roy was reborn. Although short on cash, he threw himself into community projects. He counselled young businessmen trying to get started. He did volunteer work at the local hospital. He acted as an unpaid baby-sitter so that his younger friends and neighbors could go out and enjoy themselves.

Roy is still not wealthy. But he told me recently, "For the first time, I'm really enjoying life. I only wish I had done things like this years ago."

Recently, when the back taxes on his house got beyond his means, the entire community secretly raised a fund and paid them off for him. Perhaps you read about it in the papers.

### How to Speak Directly to the Cosmic Mind That Rules the Universe

Earlier in this chapter, you discovered how to "amplify" your prayers by means of the Atomic Rites. But this method, involving as it does, prayer and meditation, is not always feasible to use in emergencies. In times of trouble, where a decision is needed on very short notice, what should you do?

Help from the Cosmic Mind is always at hand. In such a

moment, close your eyes, and ask, "What path shall I take? Please send me a sign."

When you open your eyes, the sign will be before you. Do not hesitate, but act on it immediately.

Remember one thing. This is an emergency, last-ditch technique. Do not use it all the time for minor problems, or like the boy who cried "wolf," it will fail you when you need it most.

### Your Wonderful New Future

You have now completed your study of all of the major branches of Ultra-Psychonics. You have received, if there were such a thing, the equivalent of a Doctor's Degree in the subject.

But now you must put it to use. First, discover what your cosmic mission is in life. Then, select the branches of Ultra-Psychonics that cover the area most closely, and get started.

A wonderful new future awaits you.

*THERE IS NO END — THERE ARE ONLY BEGINNINGS*

## WHAT ULTRA-SOPHOLOGY CAN DO FOR YOU

In this chapter, you've seen:

- How the Ten Actions of Joy can bring lasting happiness.
- Why Ultra-Sophology is acceptable to all religions.
- How to achieve the Great Enlightenment.
- What the Master Plan of the Universe looks like.
- How to use the Atomic Rites for riches, love, power, friendship, health and Golden Blessings.
- What the *Bardo Thodol* reveals about the Hereafter.
- How the ancient *Egyptian Book of the Dead* indicates the correct path of conduct.
- How to find your Cosmic Mission in life.
- How to get immediate help from the Cosmic Mind that rules the Universe, when you need it most.